I've been a fan of Paula Rinehart since my twenties. Her ability to combine sound, biblical theology with her sensitivity as a counselor is remarkable. This book is no exception—it's a must-read for anyone seeking to make sense of their story in light of God's greater story.

LAURA STORY, singer-songwriter

If life has turned out differently from what you expected, read this book. Paula Rinehart and Connally Gilliam skillfully write about our longings, our realities, our disappointments, and our hope for a life that's more perfect. *And Yet, Undaunted* will take you into a deeper understanding of God's Larger Story. The authors aren't afraid to ask hard questions about why a good God allows bad things to happen. You'll learn how to experience fresh faith, restored joy, and rediscovered hope as you apply Scripture to your life and find yourself surprised by God's goodness. This book is powerful, thought provoking, unsettling (in a good way), and chock-full of biblical wisdom. Don't miss it!

CAROL KENT, speaker and author of *When I Lay My Isaac Down*

These women's sage words are a beacon for those of us desperate to find him within the chaos and ache and uncertainty of our lives.

SARA HAGERTY, bestselling author of *Unseen: The Gift of Being Hidden in a World That Loves to Be Noticed* and *Every Bitter Thing Is Sweet*

In their lovely new book, *And Yet, Undaunted*, coauthors Paula Rinehart and Connally Gilliam invite women to dwell with the tension between what we long for and what is. Sharing stories from their own lives, Paula and Connally invite us to see the gospel at work, redeeming our broken lives and offering us hope we can cling to when we encounter our own sinfulness, unfulfilled dreams, and deepest losses. The gospel, with its promise of a full and future redemption, is powerfully at work now, providing the only true answer to the despair we may incline toward as we face *what is*. Tears and hope mingle in these pages, a gift to their readers.

MARIAM KAMELL KOVALISHYN, assistant professor of
New Testament Studies at Regent College

Hopeful and tender, *And Yet, Undaunted* is for anyone whose life hasn't turned out as planned or who yearns for something more. With remarkable candor and insight, the authors tell their own stories of loss and longing, asking the question we all secretly wonder: *Is God really good?* Their answer, underscored throughout the pages of this book, brought me to a new understanding of my own story and God's redemptive power in it. I highly recommend this book!

VANEETHA RENDALL RISNER, author of *The Scars That Have Shaped Me*

It's rare to find a book that encompasses gorgeous writing, authentic and hopeful storytelling, and sound biblical truth, yet Paula Rinehart and Connally Gilliam have pulled it off in their book *And Yet, Undaunted*. When life doesn't live up to our expectations and our world is full of more disappointment, pain, and suffering than we ever imagined, Paula and Connally help us see the goodness of God as it breaks through the clouds both in our present life and in God's promises for our future. If you have been longing for something more in life, pick up this book and get ready to discover what C. S. Lewis once observed: "If we find ourselves with a desire that nothing in this world can satisfy, the most probable explanation is that we were made for another world." My prayer is that this book will be read by thousands of men and women as it provides the grounded and joy-filled message we all need to hear.

DR. JOEL S. WOODRUFF, president of the C. S. Lewis Institute

Connally and Paula's writing makes my heart ache— ache for the way things ought to be and ache for the way things will, one day, be—all while dignifying the longing, disappointment, and suffering wrapped up in the now. I am so grateful for these two women: for their wisdom, honesty, and call to hopeful courage. This book will faithfully point you to Jesus as you are drawn in to engage with the deep longings and questions rumbling inside your heart.

JEN GUZI, women's leadership development, Hope Community Church

Sooner or later, and not without pain, we all come to realize that the world is not as it ought to be. We are also not as we should be. This book exposes our longings for a better world and then points us forward to the way things can and will be redeemed by Jesus Christ. Because of that, we can live realistically and joyfully—even undaunted—in this beautiful but broken world. Sharing openly about their own lives, Paula and Connally invite us to do the same and live not our best life now but our *real* life now.

BRUCE HINDMARSH, DPhil, FRHistS, James M. Houston Professor of Spiritual Theology and professor of the history of Christianity, Regent College

This wise, beautiful book will undoubtedly serve as a guide and friend through the dark valleys of life, a balm and a spur to those weighed down with regret, disappointment, and unmet longing. *And Yet, Undaunted* shows the possibilities of finding courage and joy in your life story, by pointing at the Larger Story—*what ought to be, what is, what can be,* and *what will be*—and the ways in which Love himself unites the plot and pervades each scene.

CHERIE HARDER, president of The Trinity Forum

PAULA RINEHART + CONNALLY GILLIAM

...and yet, undaunted

EMBRACED BY THE GOODNESS OF GOD
IN THE CHAOS OF LIFE

To Gloria,
Many Blessings,
Connally

NavPress

A NavPress resource published in alliance
with Tyndale House Publishers, Inc.

Blessings on
You, Gloria...
Paula

NavPress is the publishing ministry of The Navigators, an international Christian organization and leader in personal spiritual development. NavPress is committed to helping people grow spiritually and enjoy lives of meaning and hope through personal and group resources that are biblically rooted, culturally relevant, and highly practical.

For more information, visit www.NavPress.com.

And Yet, Undaunted: Embraced by the Goodness of God in the Chaos of Life

Copyright © 2019 by Paula Rinehart and Connally Gilliam. All rights reserved.

A NavPress resource published in alliance with Tyndale House Publishers, Inc.

NAVPRESS and the NavPress logo are registered trademarks of NavPress, The Navigators, Colorado Springs, CO. *TYNDALE* is a registered trademark of Tyndale House Publishers, Inc. Absence of ® in connection with marks of NavPress or other parties does not indicate an absence of registration of those marks.

The Team: Don Pape, Publisher; Caitlyn Carlson, Acquisitions Editor; Elizabeth Schroll, Copy Editor; Libby Dykstra, Designer

Cover photograph of canvas texture copyright © andersphoto/Adobe Stock. All rights reserved.

Cover illustration of watercolor copyright © Leyasw/Adobe Stock. All rights reserved.

Cover photograph of bird silhouettes copyright © satika/Adobe Stock. All rights reserved.

Photograph of Paula Rinehart taken by Tierney Farrell, copyright © 2015. All rights reserved.

Photograph of Connally Gilliam taken by Laura Merricks, copyright © 2018. All rights reserved.

Cover illustration of circle hand-drawn by Libby Dykstra. Copyright © Tyndale House Publishers, Inc. All rights reserved.

The authors are represented by the literary agency of WordServe Literary, www.wordserveliterary.com.

Unless otherwise indicated, all Scripture quotations are from the ESV® Bible (The Holy Bible, English Standard Version®), copyright © 2001 by Crossway, a publishing ministry of Good News Publishers. Used by permission. All rights reserved. Scripture quotations marked NASB are taken from the New American Standard Bible,® copyright © 1960, 1962, 1963, 1968, 1971, 1972, 1973, 1975, 1977, 1995 by The Lockman Foundation. Used by permission. Scripture quotations marked NIV are taken from the Holy Bible, *New International Version,*® *NIV.*® Copyright © 1973, 1978, 1984, 2011 by Biblica, Inc.® Used by permission. Scripture quotations marked NKJV are taken from the New King James Version,® copyright © 1982 by Thomas Nelson, Inc. Used by permission. All rights reserved. All rights reserved worldwide. Mounce Reverse Interlinear Greek-English Dictionary of the New Testament. Edited by William D. Mounce. Copyright © 2011 by William D. Mounce. All rights reserved.

Some of the anecdotal illustrations in this book are true to life and are included with the permission of the persons involved. All other illustrations are composites of real situations, and any resemblance to people living or dead is purely coincidental.

For information about special discounts for bulk purchases, please contact Tyndale House Publishers at csresponse@tyndale.com, or call 1-800-323-9400.

ISBN 978-1-63146-968-8

Printed in the United States of America

25	24	23	22	21	20	19
7	6	5	4	3	2	1

To all those who have helped us
to think and to feel our way
into such a great gospel.

I wonder what sort of a tale we've fallen into?

SAMWISE GAMGEE, *THE TWO TOWERS*

THE LARGER STORY

Once upon a time, there was a Garden. A world filled with flawless beauty and goodness, where all was right and good and whole.

We can still see so many reminders of that original goodness. Grandchildren playing in the front yard. Pink azaleas springing to life. Dinners with friends where the laughter is even better than the food. Trips to places you thought you'd never get to visit. Bike rides through beautiful green hills. Faraway places where God is doing incredible things. If there's so much goodness to be had now, how wonderful must the original world have been? This world God created that he himself said was "very good" indeed.[1]

But that goodness has been tainted. There's a worm in the apple now. Life has taken a chunk out of our hide. We all have hard things in our stories, twists and turns and sudden drops. Something is not right—really not right. It appears for all the world that God has withheld the one thing we really want. *If only.* If only what's missing could suddenly be ours, we could loosen our tense muscles, let out the breath we've been holding—a great *exhale*. Life would be complete. We

[1] Genesis 1:31.

find ourselves looking over the wall into that Garden with a hidden angst, longing for what can never be ours again.

A dark voice whispers the same old questions: *Really, can you trust what God has said—what he's doing in your life? I mean, look at the mess around you. Does God have your best interests at heart?*

Is God good? Is he really good?

Living life well—smiling at the future[2]—boils down to how we answer that question. In the face of a world that will, indeed, take a chunk out of your hide, is God good, and can we trust him?

We are two women who have wrestled with this. We have been friends for years, knocking around in the world of ministry and counseling and speaking to groups of women. We've laughed until we cried—and we've also been to hard places together.

Our personal stories are different. We've both known lost dreams, but those dreams have been as unique as our stories. Paula's family has dealt with fertility struggles. Connally has a dozen nieces, nephews, and godchildren, but she hasn't lived the daily realities of raising children. At the same time, Paula hasn't experienced Connally's world—working at an urban theological college in Philadelphia or taking the metro to a downtown-DC job at an international public-policy think tank. And while Connally's lifelong interest in racial tensions is part of our conversations, Paula has always been compassionately confounded by the topic.

---

[2] Proverbs 31:25, NASB.

As we walk through the arc of our stories in this book, you may see bits and pieces of your own. Our stories aren't anything special—in fact, they're pretty ordinary human stuff. But to answer this question of God's goodness, we all need to look our stories square in the face, to sit before the beauty of this great narrative we call the gospel and discover that our stories are part of something so much bigger. As you join us, we think you'll discover how the beautiful reality of God's goodness trickles down into the gritty places of your own life. And we believe in this truth: In your journey into God's goodness, you'll find a bedrock sense of peace—and a way to smile at the future.

WHEN GOD DOESN'T SEEM GOOD

Paula

I could hear the anxiety in my son's voice over the phone.

My husband and I were on vacation, hiking a few California trails, and I badly wanted to hear what my son was saying. So I plunked myself down on an antique bed in our cheap-but-quaint hotel room, trying to get comfortable on a mattress that sank, deceptively, toward the middle.

"Well," Brady began, "I don't want you to worry, but Hannah and I just returned from the doctor's office, and this thing of having a baby could be more complicated than we thought."

When they tell you not to worry, that's when you start to worry. "Go on," I replied, as the pit in my stomach fell to the floor.

His next words were careful. "Well, you see, there are these problems. Something is off here, not quite right there, but not to worry, not to worry, modern medicine has so much to offer. There are surgeries. Medications. In vitro procedures with catchy three-letter names."

I'm not hearing this right, I thought. Surely I was not on the phone talking about infertility with my not-yet-thirty-year-old son.

After he and his wife married a few years before, I would sit across from them at the table, staring innocently, mixing and matching their facial features to guess what their children would look like. *Beautiful children.* That was always the picture in my head. Little boys playing endless hours of Legos. Girls with pink ribbons in their jet-black hair. Sometimes I wish I hadn't seen it so clearly.

But, really, my hope for grandchildren had been shaped by a boatload of prayer. Though I've always been a bit prayer challenged, so to speak, when it comes to praying for my children, I pray like a crazy woman. And I don't stop with just my children. I have prayed, for thirty years, for my children and grandchildren and great-grandchildren. Why stop with one generation?

The prophet Isaiah inspired me in this practice. I discovered his words many years ago and have prayed them so often I know them as well as my home address: ". . . that God would pour out his Spirit on our offspring, and his blessing on our descendants, and that they would spring up among the grass like poplars by streams of water, writing on their hands 'Belonging to the LORD' and naming Israel's name with honor."[3]

As Brady explained their options for having children, these words floated through my mind, comforting me. Surely thirty years of prayer meant something in all of this. Surely God's goodness would mean that the door to this longed-for child would open in due time. Surely.

As a therapist, I hear the twists and turns of people's stories all day long. You'd think that I'd be better prepared for those moments in life when, suddenly, I wake up in a story that is mine but sure feels as if it's someone else's.

You've probably been there, right? You are flying blind. Your sense of God's goodness is threatened.

That, I've discovered, is the actual problem with life.

You and I have come smack into the middle of a story—our own story—only to discover that we aren't in control of where that story goes. We honestly didn't know we had an agenda for our life until life itself did not comply. Until our story zigged just when we thought it should zag. We are like a dazed kid who stumbles into a movie halfway through, trying to adjust our eyes to a darkened theater, wondering what is going on here. What, exactly, is the plotline in this narrative?

There are doggone-good reasons for that dazed feeling, for the days when we think we've lost our way. We are outside the Garden. And we are not yet where we're heading.

---

3 Author's paraphrase of Isaiah 44:3-5, NIV.

Think about the story you are living now. Maybe you are in the middle of that dazed feeling. You've gotten a phone call that blew you out of the water. Your perfectly good plans got flipped upside down. You woke up and wondered whose life this is. If you're honest, even if you don't feel that way right now, you've felt that way before. And you're probably going to feel that way again.

In the immortal words of the poet Madeleine L'Engle, "Someone has altered my lines. I thought I was writing this play."[4] I bet you know what she means. Our stories can be absolutely confounding at times, for two good reasons.

The Story Doesn't Go according to Script

Once, when Connally and I were speaking together in Latvia, I gave a talk about how God's goodness is reflected in the book of Genesis and how our every need and longing was completely met in the beginning. Afterward, as Connally and I sat in a café, drinking our decaf lattes, I asked for her feedback.

She hesitated for a moment, then said, "When you teach those pieces out of Genesis about how our every need and longing was so completely met in the Garden . . . the first thing I feel is anger. And then, disappointment. Honestly, I don't know what to do with this. 'Every need and longing being met' is quite far from my experience, in spite of much prayer."

Together we sat there and mourned the great gap between the world we were created for and the present reality with

---

4 See Madeleine L'Engle's well-loved poem "Act III, Scene II," which begins, "Someone has altered the script . . ."

which we contend. Our stories haven't gone according to the scripts we carried.

If you had a latte with Connally, you would probably immediately have a question about her story that you would not voice: How is this lovely, stinking-smart woman, who traipses around the planet at fiftysomething, still single when she'd like to be married?

Well, Connally would say, her unintended singleness is part of her story.

The script she was handed—as the only daughter in a southern family—definitely included a white wedding dress, a minivan of children, and a significant place smack in the center of To-Be-Expectedville, USA.

When Connally turned thirty, it hit her that she would never have toddlers in her twenties. She had dated many guys, but nothing had really clicked. How had she missed this loop called marriage? It wasn't for lack of trying.

But when her fortieth birthday rolled around—an extravaganza complete with sequined skirt and catered canapés—one friend declared, "This is like your wedding but without a groom!" Everybody (kind of) laughed, but no one missed the irony. You don't have a wedding without a groom.

Unintended singleness is only part of Connally's story, but it's a major place her tale went off script.

What script have you carried? You probably don't have to scratch very deep to find this disconcerting gap between that script you genuinely believe a good God would want to provide and the story that is your unfolding reality. Our actual lives, with disturbing regularity, refuse to follow our plans.

You Can't See What's Coming

There's another reason why we often feel a bit dazed by our lives, struggling to figure out the plots of our stories: We are creatures with limited vision.

When I was young enough to sport hair in its natural color, I assumed that women who were old enough to get their hair color from a bottle knew the ropes. Surely life didn't take them by surprise anymore. They had graduated into a special realm of certainty and insight. They had their act together.

Then I became a woman who gets her hair color out of a bottle. And I discovered that I am now only more keenly aware of my vulnerability to hard and terrible things. I have a greater repertoire of experience with the utter faithfulness of God, yes. But in crucial moments, each wild leap still feels way too much.

That's the problem with our finiteness. We are always going around a blind curve.

When my son and his wife were trying to have children, dealing with all those failed fertility treatments, our visits to their home were hard. Their house in Atlanta was just so quiet, as though the house itself ached for the pitter-patter of little feet. I felt all of this in stereo—my own losses and their losses. It felt like a double barrel of pain, some hidden cost to being a mother.

And then there were the things we couldn't see coming. A woman in Florida "chose" our son and his wife to adopt her child, who would be delivered by C-section two days after Christmas. Oh, what a party we threw!

A week before the holidays, she changed her mind.

Christmas came, as it does, whether we are ready or not. As long as I live, I won't forget gathering around that holiday table and thanking God, truly, for the baby who came. Jesus' coming was so real to us that year. How could we possibly carry such profound disappointment if, indeed, the Christ child had not come?

Two months later, we learned that the woman had faked her pregnancy. She was sufficiently overweight to pass for pregnant and collect the pass-through money from four different adoption agencies.

So many big pieces of what happens in your life, you just can't see coming.

As I grappled with all the blind alleys that infertility took our family into, I found myself sometimes singing along with one of Laura Story's first songs: "All I know to do is lift my hands to You. Take all of my life, all of my life, and *make something beautiful*."[5] Yes, that was exactly what I asked of God—that somehow he would take the broken pieces of this pain and bring beauty from ashes.[6]

I find no small comfort in what the exercise of our faith actually means to God. He knows we can't see farther than the ends of our noses. And he has not left us to fend for ourselves. We choose to trust him, though we can't see the future. We cannot see around the corner—ever. And that exercise of our faith matters to the living God. As the apostle Peter reminds

---

[5] Laura Story, "Make Something Beautiful," *Great God Who Saves* © 2008 INO Records.
[6] Isaiah 61:3, NASB.

us, this sort of faith is like gold, bringing "praise and glory and honor" at Christ's coming.[7]

In fact, the clear teaching of Scripture is that when Christ returns, he won't look for big cathedrals and throngs of people but rather these invisible places in our hearts where, against all odds, we believe and follow.

THE NEED FOR A LARGER STORY

So this is how the tale of our lives plays out. We walk far enough on the trail to discover there are twists and turns we didn't see coming. The story we are living appears to go off script. Life is uncertain. We ache for things to be made right. Or as Andrew Peterson sings in his song "Is He Worthy?,"

> Do you feel the world is broken?
> Do you feel the shadows deepen? . . .
> Do you wish that you could see it all made new?[8]

It's to this Larger Story that we now turn. All the good coping strategies and self-improvement schemes are not enough to carry us through the things we face. Life just gets too hard. But the good news is that the God who is over all of history has shown up in Jesus to redeem the future, starting now. Belonging to Jesus means that our stories have been

---

[7] 1 Peter 1:7.
[8] Andrew Peterson, "Is He Worthy?," *Resurrection Letters: Volume I* © 2018 Centricity Music.

caught up in a much larger tale-to-be-told. Our lives don't hang in thin air like a purple balloon on a skinny string.

Your story actually unfolds beneath a sacred canopy.[9] A larger frame. And if you learn to see how the real story began in the beginning—and where it's headed—you will glimpse the good heart of God that will anchor you when your world feels chaotic or your life gets crazy.

Before us is a brave new world, full of possibilities, and the miracle at the center of it all is this beautiful God who, once in history and continually still, enters our story. This is the Jesus who actually walked in our shoes. This Hero who stepped onto the stage and took the very worst part in the play. Everything you dread. All the hurt and the pain—and even death itself.

And in taking it all on, he transformed it.

The Lion of Judah allowed his roar to be silenced by sinful men—and in so doing, he gave us our true voice. He endured this death you and I will one day die, and a thousand humiliations we will face, and then turned the tables and destroyed death—which means that your life and my life can come back from the grave in a hundred ways, even on this side of heaven.

If you look at the life of Jesus closely, you will find he lived in this Larger Story we're talking about, and he is inviting us to join him there. What is this Larger Story? It is the four dramatic acts of God's redemptive story: *what ought to be, what is, what can be,* and *what will be.* And Jesus went before us. He lived within it all.

---

9 Peter L. Berger, *The Sacred Canopy: Elements of a Sociological Theory of Religion* (New York: Anchor Books, 1990).

- He was present in creation, enjoying his handiwork—this world—as it truly ought to be. This world—as it truly *ought to be*.

- He likewise experienced this sin-stained life as we do: haunted by death, with the echoes of just-missed goodness, in the fallen reality of *what is*.

- His death and resurrection simultaneously opened amazing possibilities for what life, even on this planet, *can be*.

- His promise of life to come, which is beyond all that we can think or imagine, is the guarantee of *what will be*.[10]

Here, in this Larger Story, we can find meaning and perspective and hope in our particular journey.

In my own life, I probably would have remained despondent if I thought the news my son shared on that phone call was the end of the story. I think it's true that if your story is the only reference point, there isn't much to hold on to in times of disorientation. There's nowhere to place yourself when the zigs and zags of life throw you off track.

But because you and I live inside the Larger Story, we live in the anticipation of where God will take us. An

---

[10] Many thanks to Mike Metzger, whose writing helped us see that the classic Christian categories of Creation, Fall, Redemption, and Restoration—the four-chapter gospel—can be roughly translated into the categories of *what ought to be*, *what is*, *what can be*, and *what will be*. See Michael Metzger, "Living the Gospel in Culture," Ideas for the Common Good, accessed May 27, 2019, http://208.106.253.109/essays/living-the-gospel-in-culture.aspx.

undercurrent of hope flows in the worst of circumstances. *What can be*. Redemption.

Our particular redemption showed up in another phone call, this time announcing the birth of a little girl. Sydney is her name. She is the gift of an Hispanic birth mother who chose to push past the taboo of adoption in her culture and give her child life at no small cost to herself. Sydney came to my son and daughter-in-law with a head full of black hair, making throaty little noises from the day she arrived, her own baby way to reach out and "talk."

She is now a beautiful six-year-old who throws back her head and laughs as she insists on changing her princess outfit four times a day, complete with sequin tennis shoes and an armful of bracelets. A sister and a brother have joined her.

Honestly, there are moments when these children break into big smiles and it feels like I'm peeking behind a veil. I get a tiny, heart-stopping glimpse of what Isaiah calls the splendor of the Lord.[11] And *it takes my breath away*.

I am tasting and seeing the goodness of the Lord. It comes in a different package from what I originally pictured and yet, oddly enough, that only makes me more aware of what many would call *grace*.

As we learn to trust this God we cannot control, his goodness becomes more tangible and real. Following God down paths we thought we'd never walk can be strangely liberating. And sometimes, those wild detours in our lives turn out to be the actual paths we were looking for all along.

---

[11] Isaiah 61:3, NIV.

Christians are fond of calling the gospel "Good News." We have the audacity, if you think about it, to claim that the gospel is unique, shout-it-from-the-housetops good news. Yet if that gospel shrinks to mean that Christ has come simply to fulfill my (even very good) dreams, I will end up disillusioned. If the gospel in my head is just about making life work out now, I am more lost than I know. For when the dream doesn't materialize, I will feel stranded. It will look like God has tricked me. Like he simply does not deliver. Like he is not good. And the gospel will not sound like good news at all.

If you long to journey through your story with hope, with your heart intact and able to love, you need to see yourself within the Larger Story of God. The gospel in its entirety will show you how you were created, why this world always leaves an ache, and how you can thrive within the hope of what is to come. What you do with that ache and that hope largely determines your life. But you do not walk this path alone. The power of the risen Christ will help you smile at the future, because you've been let in on the secret truth.

There is more, more, more to come.

Reflections
on
THE LARGER STORY

1. What is most engaging to you about the thought of living inside the Larger Story, where the greatness of God's goodness revealed in the gospel envelops your life? What actual difference could it make for you?

2. Paula describes several times where life has "taken [a] chunk out of [her] hide." Take a few minutes to reflect on something in your life that hasn't gone according to script, where your life has zigged when you thought it would zag.

3. In what ways have the unexpected turns in life challenged your faith in God's goodness? What brings you back to an awareness or a hope of experiencing God in the midst of life as you encounter it?

4. One of the most beautiful places in Scripture where the gospel is on display is Isaiah 55. Read through the passage on the following page, thinking about your own journey in the Lord. Where do you feel "thirst" and where do you take your "thirst"? What is God asking of you here?

> Come, everyone who thirsts,
>> come to the waters;
> and he who has no money,
>> come, buy and eat!
> Come, buy wine and milk
>> without money and without price.
> Why do you spend your money for that which is not bread,
>> and your labor for that which does not satisfy?
> Listen diligently to me, and eat what is good,
>> and delight yourselves in rich food.
> Incline your ear, and come to me;
>> hear, that your soul may live;
> and I will make with you an everlasting covenant,
>> my steadfast, sure love for David.[12]

5. We are hungry, thirsty people, lost in a broken world. In the next piece of Isaiah 55, you are hearing the plea of God's heart for us. How would you put this in your own words? What do you hear God saying?

> Seek the LORD while he may be found;
>> call upon him while he is near;
> let the wicked forsake his way,
>> and the unrighteous man his thoughts;
> let him return to the LORD, that he may have compassion
>>> on him,
>> and to our God, for he will abundantly pardon.
> For my thoughts are not your thoughts,
>> neither are your ways my ways, declares the LORD.
> For as the heavens are higher than the earth,

---

[12] Isaiah 55:1-3.

> so are my ways higher than your ways
> and my thoughts than your thoughts.[13]

6. How does this last piece of Isaiah 55 speak to where you find yourself? Where do you find comfort? Where are you challenged?

> For you shall go out in joy
> and be led forth in peace;
> the mountains and the hills before you
> shall break forth into singing,
> and all the trees of the field shall clap their hands.
> Instead of the thorn shall come up the cypress;
> instead of the brier shall come up the myrtle;
> and it shall make a name for the LORD,
> an everlasting sign that shall not be cut off.[14]

7. Perhaps the best part of the gospel is that whatever is happening in your life is never the end of the story. How does the promise of living in a much Larger Story affect the way you look at your life in the present?

---

[13] Isaiah 55:6-9.
[14] Isaiah 55:12-13.

What Ought to Be

CREATION

WHAT IF EVERY NEED we had were met or possible to meet? In the Bible, the book of Genesis paints a picture of life as our creator intended it—life without lack, where humanity was created and called to be fully connected with God, with one another, and with the creation itself. Our first parents, Adam and Eve, strolled easily with God. They were freely naked with each other. And when they weren't naming the animals, they were cultivating gardens full of beautiful and tasty fruit. Rich worship, real human bonds, meaningful work.

No wonder God declared the whole scene very good.

What might an *ought-to-be* life look like today?

The living God of the universe would be walking with you, everywhere, present as an honored Father for whom your respect and love were ever deepening. His eyes would be twinkling, and he'd smile at you like a parent with his cherished young child, or a father whose daughter danced with her groom. Your days would be filled with some amazing combination of worship and laughter, conversation and silence.

With your other friends, you could share your heart and dreams without fear—no shame, no need to watch your back. You would experience relational bonding without bondage. Your family would thrive. With men and women alike, you wouldn't have to protect your beauty, hide your gifts and talents. Unmarred, those things would pose no threat to others or invite another's ill intent.

You would live free of evil lurking at your doorstep, of fear hanging in the shadows. Innocence would reign. No broken promises; no dreams crumbling to ashes. You could count on tasting the fruit of your labor; things would really work as designed. And, at a far more mundane level, you wouldn't have to moan over your emerging double chin or less-than-sculpted arms.

By returning to an image of how things could have been, we can remind ourselves of the goodness of God's original design—of how things *ought to be*. This goodness is an integral part of our Creator God—goodness that he has designed, goodness that he longs to share, goodness that never goes away.

This memory of the Garden is a visceral knowledge that we were created for a world where all is as it should be. We were made for more than we can ever quite lay hold of in this life. This awareness alone is proof we aren't crazy when we find ourselves longing, even in the best of times, for that elusive something. To the contrary—when we listen to what our longings tell us, we are on the cusp of discovering something (and Someone) very, very good.

And so we ask this question on our journey into hope: *What do our longings reveal about the goodness of the God who created all things, including us?*

CHAPTER 1

LONGING FOR MORE

It Helps to Know You Aren't Crazy

Connally

I remember a time in my early forties when I discovered the importance of knowing and honoring the *ought-to-be* life. It was a sultry summer evening, and I'd just come from a five-o'clock church service. Taking Communion and singing corporately had been particularly sweet joys for me—moments where the veil between heaven and earth seemed to grow thin and the fragrance of eternity wafted in. As I received the bread and the cup, my worship had flowed with abandon.

Driving away from that service in my convertible, I realized that I had been refueled for the work that lay ahead of me. We have all been called to cultivate fruit just as Adam and Eve were; my current version was working for an international ministry—writing, speaking, and mentoring. And that night, after I encountered the Lord so deeply, the lifeblood for my work seemed reinvigorated.

But in that same moment, even as I felt fundamentally grateful for God's gifts, I also felt the concurrent, too-familiar twinge of unmet longing. I was—after years of praying and getting hundreds of others to do the same (and even writing a book on the topic)—still single. This didn't bother me most days anymore. But every now and then, sitting unpartnered at church touched this place in me. It was a strange irony: With my heart opened wide in the Lord's presence, my quiet, background disappointment was free to come to the light. I could stroll with the Lord in the Garden, so to speak, and I could cultivate good fruit in the world around me. But nakedness—intimacy, being *known*—with an Adam? And a family of my own? Well, all of that was perpetually elusive.

Of course I knew—intellectually, and even in a chunk of my heart—that finding a partner was not the whole story. So much relationally good, substantive human connection was woven like gold thread into my life—friends close by and around the country with whom love flowed back and forth. In that sense, I really did have the relational piece at least *halfway* there. But if I were honest, the relational gap still felt real. As if this was not how life was supposed to be, at least for me. And tonight, I felt tired of this snake pit in an otherwise beautiful Garden.

I legitimately doubted that it was purely in my power

to fill the gap, to meet my own longings. I'd done my part for the past twenty years. Worked on my stuff. Been open to date a lot of men, even when we weren't a very good fit. Recently, I'd even ventured with a friend into my first-ever speed-dating experiment at a snazzy bar.[15]

But at this moment, driving in my car, I suddenly felt the very strong pull to do anything possible to get rid of the gruesome gap. It just felt too bad. Why should I put up with this ridiculously noisy, unmet longing that I didn't have the power to fill?

I considered ways to silence the noise. Maybe that longing for a literal bridegroom needed to be totally spiritualized—I could forget flesh-and-blood guys and realize that Jesus was my husband and my ministry organization, my family. There was *some* truth in that, after all.

Or perhaps that longing for someone special to build my life with needed to be treated as dead weight, no longer meriting my time, attention, and care. Or cynically tossed—with rolling eyes and a knowing scoff—into the "cheesy" category by this smarter woman who now knew better.

But even as I contemplated these options, something else crept into my imagination: that Genesis-shaped mosaic of how life *ought to be*. It glimmered, faint at first, like gold in the light of a dim candle. But its light grew, and in no uncertain terms, it radiated its ancient, simple truth: *These longings*

---

[15] Actually, this was telling. There was the yoga lover whose joy was balancing his chakras. Next was the ex-Mormon missionary trying to find a new path. Then the handsome, divorced tennis pro who offered to give me lessons. Last was the brilliant Jewish doctor who listened to me for two minutes and told me that though I was "great to talk to," I was clearly looking for a Christian, and he hoped I could find one. He even joined me in scanning the room, and our eyes met again in recognition that the odds weren't in my favor.

for connection—with God, with others, and with creation—are right and good. I've made you for this.[16]

There was no promise of a certain kind of future. No insight into big next steps. No guarantee I'd get that for which I was made. Only the increasingly vivid reminder that wholeness came into being from the heart of our good Creator God. This was the way he'd originally designed life for his beloved image bearers. For you. For me.

It was admittedly painful to recognize that a beautiful aspect of life as it *ought to be* was frustratingly beyond my control. Perhaps you've felt this too: the pain of a genuine good always just beyond your reach. But I didn't have to excise a piece of my heart. To risk wanting that goodness— while accepting that it may not ever be mine—was not and never could be foolish. Risk meant remaining a human with an open and a living heart.

Laying my head down on my pillow that night, I realized how close I had come to buying the lie that there's no such thing as an *ought to be* in this life. The lie had such appeal. How simple it would be to tidily decide that good worship, good bonds, and good work were nice if you wanted them and could get them. But if you didn't or couldn't, no worries. Just pick the bits of the package you liked or could make happen (like worship or meaningful work), discard the rest,

---

[16] There is a God-made beauty in female union with good male strength, but—of course—not every woman on the planet wants (or needs) to get married. C. S. Lewis offers a lovely reminder in *That Hideous Strength* that many women "can bypass the male and go on to meet something far more masculine, higher up, to which they must make a yet deeper surrender." In a profound sense, Jesus really is *the consummate husband* for women and men alike. And, at a far earthier level, one only needs to know one or two married women to realize that the *idea* of marriage is not the same thing as an actual lifetime commitment to a particular man with all *his* aches and unmet longings. In other words, marriage is a good to be desired, but not a "must" to be demanded. (C. S. Lewis, *That Hideous Strength: A Modern Fairy-Tale for Grown-Ups* (New York: Scribner, 1996), 312).

and watch the gaps disappear. Cut yourself off from the achy parts of your own humanity, and then—presto!—pain gone. Move on with your life.

This lie had come so close to sounding like wisdom for the journey.

God had not shut off that desire in me that, for whatever reasons, had remained an open ache for longer than I would have ever imagined. But that meant I was actually holding on to God's gift of my own heart. That gentle, Genesis-shaped reminder had done its work, telling me that my urge to merge wasn't crazy, nor should it be unnaturally aborted. To the contrary, that reminder gave me the courage to once again offer my whole heart—gaps and all—to my creator. Then, while gratefully laying hold of the real good in my life—like a great church, a lot of friends, committed extended family, and meaningful work—I could keep moving forward.

KNOW HOW IT WAS SO YOU
CAN LIVE WELL WITH HOW IT IS

Paula

When Connally and I teach about life as it ought to be, there's a predictable reaction. We brace ourselves for it. People get angry. Frustrated. They are only more aware that their "best life now" is a far cry from what they envisioned. Good worship, relationships, and work feel like tales from another planet.

In the Garden, everything we were created for was abundantly present. And if we put ourselves into the first few chapters of Genesis, I suspect we'll find our breath taken away.

In the Garden, we know who we are. Our Father is the one who has been in relationship with the Son and the Spirit forever. Our Father is the creator. Our Father is the one who has made us, male or female, in his image.[17] From the outset, we are relational and creative, strolling with our Father in the cool of the day. Can you sense the contentment?

We stroll, too, with one another. For Adam has seen Eve and knows that "at last" he has one to whom he can hold fast. And Eve, made of the same stuff as Adam, knows the goodness of oneness with this man. They are naked, but there is no shame between them, no self-conscious preoccupation, no quiet disappointments.[18] Words like *lonely* or *lost* haven't even made it into the lexicon. Our identity is secure. Surveying the situation, our Father declares it all—and you can almost see the smile on his face—very good.[19]

But it's not just good in our relationship with our Father or each other. We are planted smack in the middle of a world where instead of fighting with the creation around us, we are blessed in our stewardship of it.[20] Imagine bluebirds, dolphins, cows, and earthworms all delighting in their place in the created world, even as we delight in them. If there were mosquitoes, they weren't biting. And our work in this garden? God's instructions are simple: Cultivate this amazing creation; bring out its fruitfulness. Multiply the edible beauty that surrounds us.[21] We get to grow tomatoes, so to speak,

---

[17] Genesis 1:26-27.
[18] Genesis 2:23-25.
[19] Genesis 1:31.
[20] Genesis 1:26.
[21] Genesis 2:9.

without the slightest threat of aphids. And we are called to turn our ripe tomatoes into a salad that would make the Barefoot Contessa proud.

Sigh. Our hearts ache for what we lost. If we stare at the here and now of our lives, we know that even our best relationships and achievements are missing something. We can see litter in the landscape of the dreams that have died. And that ache can turn to anger and frustration easily. Very easily.

There's a great temptation to just *deny the ought* of life as God intended. To pretend it doesn't matter. To numb out and take a class in French cooking. But even though we're tempted to pretend that things are okay when something inside us knows they're not, here's the truth: Pretending and avoiding is a crazymaker.

Some part of your soul knows the real scoop. Your family gatherings should indeed be glorious affairs—with no one kicking you under the table. Ministries are meant to flourish, not fall apart. Your body is literally made to bear children.

The world should not be this way.

Oh, that you could hear the heart of God echoed in your disappointment. You really aren't crazy. There's something terribly amiss. What you are dealing with is so far from God's intention that he gave his Son to transform what is to what could be.

And one day what *could* be—*will* be.

One summer, after surgeries and infertility treatments had failed, Brady and I sat on the back porch, overlooking the Appalachian mountains, both, in our own way, mourning.

For Brady, I think it felt like God had played a dirty trick on him. None of his friends had, as yet, encountered a road-block this severe. I remember saying, as though the words were put in my mouth, "You know, every single cell of my body—and yours—is fallen. Every cell bears the mark of the Fall." Eventually, that reality is inescapable.

The Fall, the brokenness of *what ought to be*, might show up as diabetes or infertility or a chronic illness. But it shows up for everyone. You aren't crazy to feel the loss.

If that Genesis story is really something more than just an old fable, your disappointment makes perfect sense. Your lament is just as it should be. You aren't crazy to feel the ache.

Rather, the ache is *the first stop on the train to hope*.

The contrast between how life *ought to be* and what happens in a fallen world can take your breath away. But the truth in that gap opens up something extraordinary: the opportunity to experience your longings—with hope, without bitterness, and without shame.

LEARNING TO LOVE YOUR LONGINGS

Years ago, I stumbled on a book called *Addiction and Grace*.[22] The author, Gerald May, wrote it mostly for the community of recovering people who suffer from a tangible addiction.

But the further I read, I realized that May was saying something more: Addiction is our universal human

---

[22] Gerald G. May, *Addiction and Grace: Love and Spirituality in the Healing of Addictions* (New York: HarperOne, 1991).

dilemma. I, me, us . . . we become overly attached to states of being, particular experiences, people whose approval we crave, familiar identities, and sometimes, a substance like alcohol or food.

In a profoundly human sense, our addictions are where our longing for the Garden shows up.

So what intrigued me was May's claim that in the recovery community, people do not make progress until they come to *love their longings.* He said that to live as a child of God is to live with love and longing, an ache for a fullness of love that's never quite within our grasp. That ache is meant to prepare us for the embrace of God. And so, in the meantime, we must come to love our longings.

To live as a child of God is to live with love and hope and growth—but it is also to live with longing, with the ache for a fullness of love never quite within our grasp. Our attitude toward that ache can prepare us for an embrace with God. We must come to love our longings.

In our longings, God is pulling us back to his original intent for us, to a deeper understanding of the Garden. As we own those longings and take them to God, we can wholeheartedly receive whatever fruitful directions he opens to us—day to day, moment to moment. Or in a phrase my recovery friends have taught me well: We take the next right step. Only in owning desire, taking it to God, and risking with others can we be delivered from the shadow world.

Loving your longings can take endlessly different shapes, but it is not an esoteric exercise:

- Perhaps you have moved to a new city and don't have anything like a sense of community there. Let the longing in this moment give you courage to seek out the community you were created for.

- Or you are painfully aware that your job doesn't remotely fit your gifts or your desires. Let your longings take you past the fear of making the phone calls that could open a door.

- Or you long for healthier, more trustworthy relationships. Perhaps for you, this means admitting to God and a friend or two that your occasional snarky comment might be cutting off the relationships you were meant to enjoy—the first step toward wholeness and trust.

LONGINGS AS A GUIDE TO HOPE

Our longings point us toward the goodness of God. When we look at how life *ought to be*—how God created it in the beginning—we see clearly that God wills our good.

Look at what he made you for in the beginning—really look there. Do you think he will leave you stranded outside the Garden forever? Will not his goodness track you down in a hundred meaningful ways? That's how the familiar

Psalm 23 ends: God will pursue you, tracking you down—not to nail your hide to the wall but to show you his goodness and mercy.[23] Now, goodness and mercy may not appear in the form you pictured, or in the time you thought was right. But your longings can keep your eyes open—because in due time, God's goodness will appear. And you don't want to miss seeing that because you stuffed all those longings away.

Loving your longings widens the lens for how you look at life. You were created for more than this world will allow you to experience. But all is not lost. There are tastes and glimmers of God's original mercy now—and that helps us trust him in places where the fog is thick and heavy. There is permission to *exhale*.

Going forward, live with one eye looking over your shoulder, a gaze that includes all that God longs to give you—his original intent for you. That gaze will steer you down the path that leads to life now. It will comfort your disappointment. You won't just stuff it all in the attic, behind the notion that you're crazy.

Though they are just the beginning of the story, your longings for *what ought to be* are essential to the journey.

---

[23] Psalm 23:6.

Reflections
on
LONGING FOR MORE

1. What does it mean to you that the life you are living is not really the world that God created you for? Where do you find hope in that?

2. Open up the Bible and read the second chapter of Genesis in a leisurely, I-am-there way. Take a few moments to let yourself walk around in that world where "it's all good," where all is as it should be. God is so immediately present in your relationships and your work. Nothing is missing. Nothing is wrong. What in this picture most strikes a note of wistful longing in you? Why?

3. What does the Garden say to you about the character of God and his original desire for your life and all humans?

4. When you realize what a far cry this world is from the life God created you for, you can either shut down your heart or let the longing drive you to God. Where have you tended to shut down desire and longing in your life? Why?

5. David said in Psalm 27:13 that he would have despaired unless
he had believed he would see "the goodness of the Lord in the
land of the living." His last words in this psalm (verse 14) are:
"Wait for the Lord; be strong, and let your heart take courage;
wait for the Lord." Can you let yourself believe that you will see
"the goodness of the Lord in the land of the living"? What does
it mean in your life to "let your heart take courage"?

What Is

FALL

WE LONG FOR THE LIFE we are created for—and those longings point us toward God's good heart for us. But reality on this side of the Garden is far tougher. We have landed on our bums here, at odds with God and one another, anxiously trying to make this thing work. In biblical language, this jarring *what is* is called the Fall. And the truth is that there are times in our lives when we so feel the burn, we wish the Fall were a fable.

The Fall means that we each hit that season of life when we realize we are not living in a bubble of protection. These seasons are dividing lines, with a "before and after." *Before my husband got really sick . . .* or *after I had a string of inexplicable miscarriages. After*, everything looks different and we don't know why. We feel stung with a fresh awareness of our own capacity to be hurt by . . . well, life.

Life is supposed to be different. Something is way off here. Paradise is ruined, and we see the dark stain everywhere we look with honest eyes. The beauty is still present—but the beauty is marred. And, most poignantly of all, the problem isn't just because of something *outside*. The beauty is marred *in us*.

The question as we journey becomes: *How might embracing the reality of the Fall catapult us deeper into God's heart and purposes?*

CHAPTER 2

GRAPPLING WITH *WHAT IS*

Outside the Garden . . . and Feeling It

Paula

When we were in our thirties, my husband, Stacy, and I packed up our two small children and headed west to Colorado. Stacy was going to lead a team that recaptured a dream for a whole Christian organization—namely, that their beautiful conference center, Glen Eyrie, might once again also be a leadership-training center.

We weren't itching to move to Colorado, despite its famous mountains. But our children settled in and fell in love with the enchanting old castle where conferences were held all summer. Training leaders in a conference-center setting had been done well here before. So Stacy and I set to work, confident that if God had led us here, the pieces would come together.

Except they didn't. After four years of effort and prayer, we looked each other in the eye and admitted defeat. Not in the rain, not on the train—even Dr. Seuss knew this was not working.[24]

Lots of people would have just gone on to the next endeavor. I wished I could. But this defeat coincided with the unraveling of my parents' solid marriage back in Virginia. These two good people I loved, whose little squabbles I'd mediated with some real success throughout my childhood, were now at terrific odds. I watched, helpless, from a distance. This new loss, alongside the end of the dream at Glen Eyrie, knocked the wind out of me.

During this season, I often felt like I had fallen into the wrong play. *These are not my lines.* I honestly felt like I had been catapulted into someone else's drama, in a role I didn't recognize. This could not be my life.

It took me quite some time to realize that the noise of my world cracking apart was actually the sound of me busting through my illusions of immunity. I might be saved by grace, but for the first time, I could feel reality hit me: I wasn't going to get a pass. The world is not as it should be, and—deep breath, deep breath—anything can happen to any of us. That realization is what it means to get, emotionally, that you are outside the Garden.

For some people, this shock is only a vague disquiet, and for others, like myself, it's more like being slapped upside the head. But the truth is, no one avoids this rite of passage.

---

[24] Dr. Seuss, *Green Eggs and Ham* (New York: Random House, 1960).

Not really. It is our human habit of the heart, left over from childhood, to wrap ourselves in the illusion that we live in protected space. We think our family background or education or God himself—something—will keep the fallenness of a fallen world from actually touching us deeply. But nothing does.

I remember putting words to this experience with a man whose first wife had died after a battle with breast cancer, leaving him with four school-aged children. He had later remarried, and his wife, Priscilla, was my good friend. So one night, while she loaded the dishwasher, I unloaded on Doug.

"You know, this is not what I pictured would happen when we came to the Glen to do this leadership center."

Doug looked at me for a long minute. And then he said, "You didn't think it would look like what you pictured, did you?"

Oh yes, I thought it would turn out like I envisioned—wasn't that what it meant to believe the promises of God? And you better believe I had Bible verses to back all that up.

He looked at me for an even longer minute. "Sometimes it works out better than you could imagine, Paula. And sometimes it's worse. But it hardly ever looks like the picture in your head."

Oh.

I had held the script of my life with a death grip. I had Bible stories and glorious verses to substantiate all that. But the story was also an agenda, one that didn't take into account reality in a fallen world. Even good relationships can falter, and the best-laid plans can turn to ashes.

That was a new beginning for me, one that could only happen once my illusions bit the dust: I saw that trusting God means I don't have my sticky little fingers glued to a particular outcome. That was a sea change for me. But the more I let go of an agenda, the more the storm within subsided. Slowly, the world began to look different.

OUR LIVES AS LIVING PROOF

The poet Walter Wangerin once said that he knew Christianity was a religion that talked a lot about death and resurrection—he just didn't realize that, at points, it would actually *feel* like death.[25]

Our lives provide an experiential proof of the theology that's woven in from the first pages of the Bible to the last. We are making our way from the Garden of Eden . . . to the City of the Living God. And there's lots of loss and death and sin in between. In fact, your *awareness* of that reality is living proof. The Bible describes life *as it actually is*—with the hope for what it can be in Christ.

It's not fashionable to talk about the Fall even among people of faith, to acknowledge that every aspect of life as we know it bears the brunt of our basic rebellion against God. We talk about creation, redemption, and restoration but fast-forward past that second act so riddled with grief and sin.

How else, though, do we make a particle of sense of the child who spends fifteen years rotating through temporary

---

[25] Walter Wangerin, *Reliving the Passion: Meditations on the Suffering, Death, and Resurrection of Jesus as Recorded in Mark* (Grand Rapids, MI: Zondervan, 1992).

foster homes when a couple was dying to adopt him at three? How do we wrap our heads around the wife who leaves a pretty decent husband and children for the high-school boyfriend who suddenly reappears in her life via Facebook?

How else do you explain some of the things that have happened to *you*? Or those you love?

Even in the stinging awareness that we are outside the Garden—and not yet home—something in this acknowledgment of *why* is an odd comfort and validation of reality.

As I've grieved the impact of the Fall in my own life, I've found myself turning to a woman's story in the Bible that feels utterly contemporary. I can picture myself being one of this woman's good friends. I get her—and I know she'd get me.

This woman has clear hopes for her life—but then everything falls apart. She finds herself in a foreign land; her husband is dead, her sons are dead, and she's staring in the faces of daughters-in-law who "aren't her people," as the saying goes. Her name is Naomi.

She's had such a blasting dose of the Fall that loss is all she can see. Life can feel like that on a string of bad days. Naomi doesn't sugarcoat anything. When she returns home to Israel and everyone is happy to see her alive, she insists that she needs a name change. "Call me Mara," she says, which means "bitter."[26] She's convinced God has dealt her a bad hand. There's no future for her.

That's how living in the wrong world actually feels. Your

---

[26] Ruth 1:20.

field of vision narrows. Everything is uncertain. It feels impossible to trust even the positive stuff happening right under your nose.

When I read the book of Ruth, I linger for a while in the end of Naomi's story. The last act of the drama shows Naomi sitting on the stage, rocking a baby. Her friends are laughing and celebrating this new baby on her lap. In the plate full of brown rice that has been Naomi's life, here is a sweet piece of Godiva chocolate. Naomi has absolutely no idea that King David and the Messiah himself will come through this child. She doesn't know anything more about the threads of glory God is weaving out of the broken strands of her life. He is always doing more in our stories than you or I know is happening.

Naomi's story helps me rightsize my expectations about life. *It can get pretty rough.* But there are a thousand things God is doing when all I can see are closed doors, empty in-boxes, and a broken heart.

When you are grappling with your vulnerability in the middle of *what is*, it seems, at least for a while, like the bottom is falling out of your life. It's an honest-to-goodness free fall. All that vulnerability feels like dependency and weakness.

But it's in your vulnerability that you discover God is there, whether you feel his presence in the moment or not. His arms will catch you. You won't be left orphaned by the side of the road. You will be held more tightly than you know.

And that is the strange thing. As life or God or the death of dreams wrests the script out of your hands, and you learn that dependency means you are held, you can almost hear yourself exhale. You can feel a fresh breeze blowing through open windows. The rumor of hope is in the air. You start to suspect that the Good News might be better news than you thought.

Perhaps—just perhaps—you could risk believing that this God who came in the flesh is good in ways you had not thought to imagine.

WE ARE VULNERABLE

Connally

After I'd written the book *Revelations of a Single Woman: Loving the Life I Didn't Expect*, person after person seemed to expect that God would then, *finally*, step in and deliver the goods (meaning "husband"). I'd obediently written the book that I was called to write. Now I would get my reward.

Around this time, a few girlfriends and I acknowledged over a glass of wine that there was *no way* we could change, create, or control men into being who we wanted them to be. (Well, we were acknowledging that in principle, if not yet practice.) I invited them to join me in fasting and praying one mealtime a week for three things: marriage for those who wanted to be married; courage for men to stand upright and walk into relationship; and courage for women to see where we need to change and then to change.

At first, my two friends balked. It's a slightly embarrassing bummer to think that this thing that most women have done naturally for eons—getting married and having children—is now demanding *our prayer and fasting*. Could the *what is* of our lives really be that, well, pathetic? But within a few months, we were all on board. What started as a weekly group-email reminder among friends grew over time to a blog-led, large-group, fast-and-prayer time. Over the course of about eight years, our minimovement embraced ten primary writers, two generations of leadership teams, and maybe two thousand participants from around the world.

Amazingly, the skipped Monday lunches and the weekly prayer sessions seemed to birth story after story of women whose faltering dreams of marriage and family had suddenly, as if out of nowhere, been realized. One friend suggested early on that our prayers were like the small iron tools that carved chinks in rocks, cracks into which God could pour his powerful Spirit.

One biblical Greek word for God's power is *dunamis*, from which we get the word *dynamite*.[27] And we seemed to see the hard places of disappointment and hopelessness in women, and passivity and fear in men, blown up. Even now, I'm in awe of some of those stories.

Old boyfriends reappearing from nowhere. Porn habits coming to light and being wrestled down. Unwanted sexual pulls diminishing. Fear of marriage melting away. Plus, women who had felt so deeply alone and powerless in their singleness now seemed to find courage and camaraderie. It was amazing. Perhaps the icing on the cake was that everyone in the original leadership team, all in their late thirties or

---

[27] Bible Tools, "Bible Verses about Dunamis," accessed May 30, 2019, https://www.bibletools.org/index.cfm /fuseaction/Topical.show/RTD/CGG/ID/4130/Dunamis.htm.

early forties, got married and had children. Well, all but one of us.

That would be me.

Seriously.

I'm not kidding.

One day, I realized that I was the only unmarried blog writer left. Aching and incredulous, I beseeched our heavenly Father, "God, how is it that you give me this idea, and everyone else gets married and has children? What are you thinking? How is this fair?"

With a touch of quite earnest melodrama, I realized I felt like Moses. He had led the people to the Promised Land, but he himself did not go in. In a moment of angry mistrust, he had taken a stick and smashed the rock—the rock out of which God had promised water. And that outburst cost him Promised Land entry. I just didn't get it. "God, what is up? Is there some big rock I smashed with a stick? And even if I am a rock smasher, what about grace?"

God's response? Crickets.

Actually, the word *crickets* is not fair.

I think God was speaking. Had been speaking. And was continuing to speak. And act. More than ten years after we began praying that prayer, I realize that for me, he has undeniably answered part three of our ongoing prayer: that women, including me, would recognize where we need to change and then change.

My change? Well, as this sustained singleness thing (with its disappointing pains and its surprisingly freeing lessons and undercurrents) has shown me, I do not control men (or women for that matter), nor do I ultimately control my destiny. This is not negating the reality of wise and foolish choices. And it's certainly not a fatalistic assertion that I'm simply a victim of others' choices. I have agency, and I can (and am even called to) pray, plan, and act. We all are. All of us have meaningful relationships and work to embrace.

But simultaneously, an inescapable, concurrent reality exists: The world has more muscle than any one of us does. This world does not have to obey our dreams. Life lived on this fallen planet can and often does stamp a resounding *no* on our most-longed-for *yes*.

Ugh. Sometimes I just hate this reality. I often want to reach for the remote control, fumbling to change the channel. But it's as if even the sweetest Hallmark movie has a dark side to it: We can close our eyes, but we can't fast-forward.

This is the *is* of fallen life that every bone in my body has fought—not just in the world of men and relationships or even family and friendships but in struggles at work, church, national politics, and tough medical diagnoses, or in far more mundane things like missed flights and frozen computers. And I have fought accepting the world as it really is in large part because such a reality means I ultimately don't have the power to *not get hurt*.

I am, fundamentally, as Paula has discussed, vulnerable.

The Latin word from which we get our word *vulnerable* is *vulnerare*, which means "to wound, hurt, injure, maim."[28] We

---

[28] Online Etymology Dictionary, s.v. "vulnerable (adj.)," accessed May 30, 2019, https://www.etymonline.com/word/vulnerable.

are people who, living in a sin-soaked world, can (and will) be wounded. No wonder we default to using every available skill and Bible verse to dodge this fact.

Being hurt—whether it shows up in the face of an absentee parent or an angry child, at the hand of an arrogant boss or an aggressive perp, or simply in the nicks and cuts of daily disappointments—feels so bad. None of us wants stomach-dropping anxiety or heart-racing fear. Our vulnerability is an irrefutable reminder that life is not the way it *ought to be*. The good guys do not always win. We are not in the Garden.

But this is where the story gets interesting.

When we recognize that we are inescapably naked and not just a little afraid, we suddenly receive the strangest of invitations.

Do you know how it feels to receive actual paper, sent-in-the-mail invitations to festive events? Whether with polka dots or expensive engraving, such invitations fill me with a feeling of anticipation blended with belonging. There's a beautiful "thing" out "there" with "them," and I get to go!

This is *not* the kind of invitation I'm talking about.

No, this invitation is often a quiet, intangible whisper in the silence, when the "thing" out "there" with "them" has crumbled away. It's as if someone calls your name in the dark of night, while you're half-asleep. The Whisperer says, "Come *with me*." No polka dots; no engraving; no mention of a time, date, or duration. *With me.* And that is the core of the invitation—an invitation to move forward into reality *with Jesus*.

THE RICH YOUNG RULER

Of course, we don't always respond to the invitation. We can conclude we're hearing things and just roll back over. Or perhaps awakened and up, we put our hands on our hips, declare that *what is* stinks, reassert that life ought to be different, and pledge to find our way back to the Garden on our own, thank you.

The rich young ruler in the Bible reacted just this way.

Though I am neither rich, nor young, nor a ruler, I feel for this guy. His way with spiritual matters seems, well, so twenty-first century, so North American. He is the one who, seemingly in search of a greater sense of this "with-God-ness," asks Jesus what he must do to inherit eternal life. You perhaps know the story. Jesus lists a few of the Ten Commandments, and it's easy to imagine this fellow nodding. *Check. Check. Got it. Yep.* These are realities he can live with.

Maybe you can imagine the contemporary American Christian version: *Pursue spiritual formation, be nuanced in your speech (avoid Christian clichés), seek justice and community, find a meaningful vocation, love God and people and don't be a hater.* Or perhaps the not-particularly-Christian version might sound something like: *eat sustainably, recycle (single-stream doesn't count), do hot yoga, find a meaningful vocation that pays well, love people but don't be a hater.* You get the idea. Instructions that seem manageable. Doable.

I can almost see this guy nodding, chill and confident, as he asks, "All these I have kept. What do I still lack?"

Then Jesus offers an audible invitation: "Sell what you possess and give to the poor, and you will have treasure in heaven; and come, follow me."[29]

This is the mic-drop moment. The Whisperer is now speaking aloud the words that this man needs to hear. *Follow me into reality, even if it means jettisoning all that gives you the illusion of protection.*

Some of us have had our illusions of control stripped away for as long as we can remember. *What is* has been hard from the beginning, and not by our own choice. For others, such understanding has come later in life, perhaps slowly. But here, Jesus is simply and directly asking this rich young man to deliberately abandon any illusions of control. Not a stripping, but an ungripping. An invitation to face *what is* with *him*. It's a risk, of course.

This young man hears the *with me* invitation, but he is not stupid. Possessions can provide protection. Pleasure. Power. Possibilities of managing one's vulnerability. This fellow appears to do a quick cost-benefit analysis, and he answers Jesus with his feet: "He went away sorrowful, for he had great possessions."

We don't know how the story goes from there. The rich young ruler falls out of the pages of Scripture as quickly as he entered them. When he walks away, though, he is sorrowful. He has been given—confronted with, really—a profoundly tough choice by Jesus: Choose a way forward in life *with stuff* or *with me*. So he makes his choice.

---

[29] Matthew 19:20-21.

I wonder if he recognizes the irony as he leaves. Already in that moment, the *stuff* is proving a poor buffer to life's hurt. His vulnerability hasn't disappeared. To the contrary, the proverbial snake in the grass slithers in this young man's self-made garden; the reality of sorrow goes with him.

WAIT, WHY ARE WE TALKING ABOUT THIS?

The Fall has left us vulnerable. When we look at life as it really *is*, our intrinsic vulnerability inevitably reveals itself. We're naked and afraid, and probably lunging for control. But if we face reality, if we acknowledge *what is*, we can discover something else as well: the Whisperer's invitation to come "*with me.*"

If I tune my ear, I can hear his words echo in the air. Maybe they are quiet; maybe they are loud. Maybe they are subtle; maybe they are direct. But for the life of me, and maybe even despite me, such words begin sounding like ones that are worth my attention. *With me*, he says.

Knowing Jesus, going with him around the blind curves of a sin-bent world, is an invitation so good that our illusions of self-sufficiency pale in comparison. His invitation beckons us forward, deeper, and further along in our trek toward that which really is beyond what we could ask for or imagine. This invitation is into the never-ending life that the rich young ruler was after in his heart of hearts.

Looking life in the eye—as it *is*—can free us to acknowledge that, *Yes, despite our savviest skill sets and our most persevering prayers, our lives are filled with fragments of lost dreams, failed relationships, unfair outcomes, surprising sorrows, and a host of subpar strategies for control.*

But beneath the broken pieces of our hearts and lives, we also find an invitation: to stand on the Rock beneath our feet. Beneath the jagged shadows of this world, our toes will find a solid and strong place to touch down.

On him. With him.

Again and again. And again.

Reflections

on

GRAPPLING WITH *WHAT IS*

1. When did you first become aware—or when are you most aware—that something is deeply amiss, that the Fall has invaded your life too? How might embracing the reality of the Fall catapult you deeper into God's heart and purposes?

2. You aren't the author of the story you are living. You contribute, but you don't have as much control as you'd like. How has the awareness of *not* really being in control affected you at various points in your life? Are there times when that has driven you to God? If so, what caused your awareness? Where did that journey take you?

3. Naomi never pictured herself as a widow living in another country, the mother of two dead sons. She returned home with her daughter-in-law in tow, and her old friends couldn't believe it was her. How was Naomi's perspective of life and of God altered by a deep dose of the Fall? When have you experienced the temptation to let difficult circumstances and hard losses shape your emotional understanding of God?

4. I love the story of Naomi. God gives us a peek behind the curtain. Naomi's story ends with her holding her grandson, surrounded by her friends and celebrating God's goodness. If you think about the story that God is writing in your life, how does Naomi's story give you hope?

5. In our vulnerability, we search for a means to feel safe, protected, and in control. Just as he did with the rich young ruler, Jesus bids us to come to him. As Connally wrote, "Follow me into reality, even if it means jettisoning all that gives you the illusion of protection." What does this mean in your life?

6. Our ultimate hope is that, despite all the vulnerability that comes from living in a world of loss and hardship and injustice, *we get to do life with God*. We are not left to our own devices. Picture in your mind the places or situations where you feel most vulnerable. As you sit with that picture, take these words from Proverbs into that picture of vulnerability:

> Trust in the LORD with all your heart,
>   and do not lean on your own understanding.
> In all your ways acknowledge him,
>   and he will make straight your paths.[30]

7. What things within you—for example, places of renewed peace, creativity, or gratitude—begin to shift as you lean on this God who, as in the rich young ruler's story, sees you . . . and loves you?

---

[30] Proverbs 3:5-6.

CHAPTER 3

NAKED, AFRAID, AND NOT SO NICE

Sin Is Not a Dirty Word

Connally

A friend of mine once wore a T-shirt with these French words: *La vie est dure. Dieu est bon.*—Life is hard. God is good.

God is good. Oh, yes. Our toes really can touch down on this solid truth. But, yes, also, life is hard. The world is a tough place because it is fallen. There really are obstacles of rubble and deep, gray shadows through which any of us will pass as we journey. In all our mental life maps, we can expect to find swamps with warning signs, forests that should have been marked by skulls and crossbones.

Even for those of us like me who would prefer a life of Broadway musicals, an honest assessment of *what is* reveals that not everything in life will come up roses and daffodils.

And here's the sometimes tougher (and yet, ultimately free-ing, concurrent) truth: Fallenness doesn't just spring up at us from *out there*. In the second act of the gospel, facing *what is*, we must also face what is *in us*.

MY WILL BE DONE

I'm sitting on a plane, flying cross-country, and the man next to me is snoring. Not just snoring, but deeply, problemati-cally, profoundly snoring. Gasping, really—it's an arrhythmic cadence that sounds like gravel pouring down a hollow pipe. I find myself wondering if maybe he needs medical attention. And incapable of concentrating on any of my work, I find myself, frankly, wanting to slap him into silence.

Like many people, I've learned that much of my spiritual growth has come because I've needed God. I am, in fact, *quite* vulnerable, able to get hurt. Much of my discovery of the fallenness of the world has happened because of the bro-ken pieces falling down on me, and I've sought God for his loving-kindness in presence, protection, and provision.

But we'd be doing God's big Story a gross injustice if we didn't mention the other part of the Fall: *It, they, them, he and/or she* are not the only problems in this world. *I* am also the problem.

The unfashionable but robustly good phrase for what I'm talking about here is *personal sin*. Sin is in part a shorthand explanation of those things that roll through the world and over us. It leaves us broken and needy, muddying our every step with shame.

But the Fall brings something else as well. It doesn't just show up as the part of me (and of us all) that wants to slap the snoring madman on the plane or smack God's rock in thirsty, fearful frustration. It is also the piece in each of us that holds up a fist to God and declares, perhaps in words that only he can hear, *My*—not *thy*—"will be done, on earth as it is in heaven."[31]

Years ago, I sat in a basement-level college classroom, discussing John Milton's classic work *Paradise Lost*. When I read those famous-for-centuries words put in Satan's mouth by Milton, the assertion that it is "better to reign in Hell, than serve in Heav'n,"[32] something in me froze. The fallen angel and I were far more alike than I'd dare admit.

COMING OUT OF DENIAL

Many of us have experienced painful life circumstances, and when we speak about the chaos of life around us, we often use words like *broken*. We are right to do so because much of *what is* is broken; far too often, God's original goodness ends up twisted in nasty knots or flat out chopped in two. And because we do not want to be considered judgmental (which contributes to suffering rather than relieving it), when we speak about the chaos of life around us, we often feel a strong pull to bypass this idea of personal sin. Such sin talk seems the purview of a bygone era, populated by seventeenth-century writers like John Milton. Or perhaps

---

[31] Matthew 6:10.
[32] John Milton, *Paradise Lost* (London: Penguin Books, 2003), book 1.

now the language of personal sin characterizes the oppressive, the self-righteous, the decidedly uber-religious types. How then could talking about it help anything?

So when I consider the painful chaos of *what is* in this life, I too easily snuggle down into an unspoken working hypothesis: *Except where life has been a bit tough and caused cracks, leaving you or me a genuine victim, fundamentally, I'm okay and you're okay.* The only real problem is the vague *them*—those people from the other political party, opposite side of the tracks, part of the family, or end of the pew who have created all these problems. And if *they* could just be fixed, perhaps through more education or better policies, all would be well.

The problem with this working hypothesis is that it's not grounded in reality. And as counterintuitive as it may sound, holding on to this seemingly chilled-out *I'm okay; you're okay* (*even if* they *aren't*) perspective isn't the path to freedom. Denial never is.

Let me flesh this out.

In my early elementary-school years, I had tender-hearted friendships with a number of boys and girls of different ethnicities. This was the simple by-product of the school my parents placed me in. At the same time, my life was gently woven in at a heart level with some black women like Hester Houston and Essie Mae Smith. I did not know at the time that these were special voices.

As I passed through my teens and twenties, I discovered more and more about the tough racial history and current realities in the world around me. My discovery as a young, preppy white woman was piecemeal. I worked with biracial ministries; I worked on racial-reconciliation efforts; I worked as a minority for a few years at an urban theological college; and I grew in a variety of multiracial friendships. Throughout the journey, this exposure—along with the good voices of my youth and the reshaping influence of God's Word—rang out the truth that all people were created in the image of God. Each one of us, no matter who we are, is equal before Jesus Christ.

But at the very end of the day, as true as I knew these declarations to be, such truths seemed to penetrate only so far. In the quiet shadows of my interior landscape, in regions almost inaccessible to me, I began to realize that I still carried an attitude, a way of looking at the world that was, for lack of a better term, culturally arrogant. You might call it snobbish. You might call it (wince) racist. It definitely smacked of expecting to reign (albeit quietly) near the top of the social heap. Nobody had ever deliberately taught me to think this way. But I had grown up silently recognizing that in my world, being a white, economically resourced southerner equaled *culturally more powerful*. And in spite of all my knowledge to the contrary, *culturally more powerful* translated almost without thought for me into *intrinsically better*.

When I had flashes of this attitude in myself, though, I was mortified. Intellectually, I knew so much better. Such attitudes were wrong. And emotionally, I recoiled at the shame of being thought an elitist or racist. How could this messed-up, arrogant vision be mine? So as soon as my dark thoughts poked up their ugly heads, I shoved them down before anyone could see. I might not be able to extirpate the ugliness, but such thoughts could not be allowed to become public. I knew they were displeasing to God, and I also knew they might reveal that I wasn't intrinsically better than anyone else. And where would that leave me? The *what is* inside of me simply couldn't be allowed to show itself.

It is in this kind of context where the *I'm-okay-you're-okay* perspective proves useless at best and creates bondage at worst. When the ugliness of my personal sin confronts my conscience, particularly if we're all supposed to be fundamentally okay, it triggers a frenzy to cover up. Who wants to risk showing up as an alcoholic at the teetotalers' gathering? When "being okay" or "being a nice person" is the cultural given, the guilt and shame of not measuring up can send me, like any of us, scurrying into hiding. I'm going to shove that junk into the deepest corner, finding a fig leaf big enough to cover my sin and green enough to still look good.

The problem, however, is that hiding behind even a big, green fig leaf makes things worse! Denial leaves me more and more isolated, and sin remains, continually tainting me and those I bump into.

Dietrich Bonhoeffer, a German theologian who fought against Hitler, put it this way: "He who is alone with his sin is utterly alone. . . . Sin wants to remain unknown. It shuns the light. In the darkness of the unexpressed it poisons the whole being of a person."[33]

---

[33] Dietrich Bonhoeffer, *Life Together* (New York: Harper, 1954), 112.

It was a profound gift, then, that God dropped Maria and me into the same house as roommates for four years. More often than not, only relationship can coax us out of denial, bringing the reality of our sin to the light. And that happened with me and Maria.

Initially, I showed up in that house with all the right answers about race. White and woke. Likewise, Maria, as an African American, came with a host of white friends. And probably in about two minutes of meeting each other, we had each sensed the cracks in the other's story. Maria smelled in me my latent ethnic arrogance. Likewise, I smelled her residual mistrust of white people, no matter how many friendships she pointed to in protest. We aspired to be Christian sisters prayerfully pursuing the harmony that we knew Jesus wanted between us. But in fact, *what is* meant we were more like tigers, ready to pounce.

Most prominently, despite my words about Jesus as my source of identity, it became clear as Maria and I circled each other that my deepest sense of personal value was inextricably tied to social status. Where I ranked was who I was. A pretty wobbly and exhausting way to gain and maintain a sense of self, no doubt. But dig deep enough, and it was mine.

Slowly, I realized my bind, pinging between pride and shame and fearing the revelation of either. On one hand, my heart harbored the unacknowledged suspicion that my people's historic power was proof of our intrinsic superiority. Maria felt that suspicion in me. Simultaneously, I feared that perhaps I was intrinsically worse than people of color.

Maybe my white privilege was just the product of arrogance specifically endemic to my people?

On top of all of this, I had some strange notion that as a black woman, Maria could, like a priest, release me from this icky bind if only she'd grant me impunity. Somehow, because she was black, if she could approve of me, she could pronounce me good. My pride would disappear and my shame would melt. Of course, this meant she couldn't be just Maria, a regular human being, a friend with strengths and weaknesses. And that pressure created its own problems.

In the midst of all of this, she tried to be okay, and I tried to be okay. But we weren't okay.

Eventually, the tigers pounced.

Unleashed in one utterly uncharacteristic screaming fight, our un-okay-ness ripped through each other's big, green fig leaves, unearthing in each of us the ugly lies that were buried deep in our interior spaces. She told me the truth about myself, calling out my attitudes for what they were—not just ignorant, not just a product of my own brokenness, but *sin*. Personal sin embedded in me that was painful to her and an offense against our shared heavenly Father. (I called out a few things, too, with her, but that is her tale to tell.)

The journey together wasn't easy or straightforward. There were difficult words. Wincing moments. Awkward pauses. Truth telling. Wound licking. Prayer. The discovery that my sin was not just against her but also against our shared creator. Repentance. Forgiveness. Attitude shifts. Mix up the steps and repeat.

Energized by our shared conviction that in the blood of Jesus, we really could and should enter something approximating true sisterhood, we just kept fighting our way forward. Facing our wounds and our sin. It helped that we also both happened to be as stubborn as mules.

Slowly, haltingly, as God's Spirit continued to flow in, fresh waters began pushing out the brackish binds. I'll never forget Maria shaking her head almost in disbelief as we looked back on this time: "Something in you became different," she noted. "Before, it felt like I was somehow supposed to be in the kitchen and you in the dining room. Since then, I've known that we're in there together." It was as if the floodwaters that were released when the dams of denial broke open between (and within) us catapulted us onto a new relational path.

So much more could be said, but here is the bottom line: Without this tough confrontation with *what is*, this naming of sin as sin, something so real never could have emerged between Maria and me. Right answers and good intentions are never enough in the face of the ugly parts of us that want, like Satan himself, to reign as god. But when *what is* is named honestly in the presence of God (and, more often than not, another person), things as gruesome as misplaced identity or cultural arrogance—or whatever else might be creeping around your deep interior space—can be named, forgiven, and dislodged. I think that's just another name for confession. And when we risk confessing the truth about what really is, amazingly, the actual *what is* can begin to change.

THE GIFT OF BEING SEEN

I could give many more examples of the hidden ugly in my life. I suspect you could too. But the point isn't the length or depth of a catalog of personal flaws. It's not about a hyper-scrupulous, never-ending self-inventory. That's not what God has asked of us. His priority is cleaning away the mold of our souls so that he might make his home with his people and we with him (and one another) forever, usually starting in our real-life, right-now circumstances.

I cannot think of a better example of this than the story of Jesus and, as she is referred to by the Gospel writer Luke, a "woman of the city."[34] Read: Prostitute. Hooker. I'm sure many had hard words for her. But that's where she had landed. And everyone knew it.

This woman of the city, however, has apparently encountered Jesus before. The encounter must have been compelling, for when she finds out that he is eating at the home of Simon the Pharisee, a prominent religious-community leader, she bursts into the dinner party to anoint Jesus' feet with her precious alabaster jar filled with ointment. What ensues is a hot mess of tears and hair, as she kisses his toes and anoints his feet.

Think about this for a moment. Who barges into a dinner party hosted by those who disdain you? Who then, crying, collapses in honor at the feet of the honored guest? What must have been driving her?

---

34 Luke 7:36-50; "woman of the city": verse 37.

The entire scene seems surreal. If it were to happen today, the whole thing would be all cell phones and security guards. Instead, she gets the attention of God in the flesh.

Linger in the story, and you start to realize that this God in the flesh, Jesus, is completely and lovingly focused on this woman of the city. Jesus sees all of who she is. Of course, the party's host thinks the encounter between this woman and Jesus reveals Jesus' blindness. Simon, the Scriptures say, muses to himself, "If this man were a prophet, he would have known who and what sort of woman this is who is touching him, for she is a sinner." But Simon is about to get an eye-opener.

With this woman pouring out her heart, tears, and oil at his feet, Jesus tells a short story about debt cancellation and love. There are two people, one with a small debt and one with a large one, and both had their debts forgiven. Who, asks Jesus, would love the forgiving creditor more? Simon answers quickly: The person with the bigger debt would love more. Bingo.

"Do you see this woman?" Jesus asks Simon. Luke doesn't record an answer. But you can almost hear a pin drop. In a seemingly slow and repetitive cadence, Jesus then continues, making his point:

You gave me no water, *but she* gave me her tears.

You gave me no kiss, *but she* has not ceased kissing me.

You gave me no oil, *but she* has anointed me.

Water to cleanse, kisses to honor, oil to anoint—all the gifts a host would offer an honored guest. And only this woman of the city, this sinful woman, gave these gifts to Jesus. This one who had played host to so many men in all the wrong ways is now publicly honored as the loving host of the God of the universe.

Simon, do you see?

But Jesus isn't just offering Simon an aha moment about his own lack of love. No, Simon's story is simply the subplot. After linking this woman's big outpouring of love to her recognition of her forgiven debts, Jesus declares aloud—for all around the table to hear—"Your sins are forgiven. . . . Your faith has saved you; go in peace."

The Lord of the universe has met this woman of the city as she really is, in all her public shame and personal sin. He has seen *what is*. He has loved her. She has been set free to go in peace.

And she is honored. Not just in a private spiritual moment, but in front of her judges. Nothing to hide. No longer afraid.

Can you imagine what she might have felt?

Those dinner guests now start to talk about Jesus. *Um, who does this Jesus think he is—forgiving sins?* You can almost see them lose themselves in nervous speculation about the theo-political implications of his words. But she, the one who has found herself in self-abandon, slips away unnoticed.

Watching her in my mind's eye, I realize that this "not nice" but terribly tough and tender woman is a hero to me. She doesn't wince at having the truth about her seen or told. She doesn't recoil at the prospect of needing Jesus' offer of forgiveness. She doesn't pretend to be more or less whole or broken, holy or sinful than she really is. What matters to her is, simply, what is real. Eyes wide open, she looks beyond the furrowed brows of those who do not see her and into the eyes of him who really does. And amid the messy jumble of tears and love and truth and forgiveness, Jesus—God in the flesh—brings her home to peace with himself. Jesus sees—and loves—all of her.

I love this story. We're never really told what her tears are about: seemingly some mysterious combination of her repentance and her love for and from Jesus. I'm not even sure which comes first, the repentence or the love. It's all in there in a messy, beautiful puddle. And this gives me courage—to know that when I show up in a muddling mix of tears, repentance, and love for Jesus, he is right there. Others may or may not get me, but he sees, forgives, and loves me fully. *Loves me fully.* Perhaps that sounds too pietistic, too individualistic. Too much about Jesus and Connally. We know the story is much bigger than that. But it's not smaller than. And it's one hundred times better than some vague denial about you being okay or me being okay. For when you or I bring to Jesus the God's-honest-truth about what really *is* in our lives—including the hidden (or not so hidden) ugly parts—it really can set us free to move, undaunted, down new paths.

SEEING *MY* FACE IN THE CROWD OF *THOSE* SINNERS

Paula

When you know that Jesus knows there is something not right in you—something twisted and broken and dark—and yet he sees you and loves you into a new place, everything changes. The Cross makes possible something extraordinary: You are known as you actually are—and still loved.

God has a way of taking me past the veneer and that mental list of *things I've done wrong in life* to an awareness that's far deeper. The one who sees me and my sin has, by his own merit, paved my path home.

But still, there is a girl inside of me, and her fist is in the air. She's not singing "Just as I Am." She's belting out "My Way"[35]—she wants to do things the way she wants to do them because even though she gave her life to Jesus and all that, it's her life. Right?

My way of doing things has been to fashion a life that means something—like, really means something. It's that illusive mirage of *significance*, though the word feels inflated even as I write it. The strange part is that my need to be *somebody* got all tangled up in my relationship with Jesus.

This may be hard to believe, but one distinctly cool way to rebel in my generation was to become a serious Christian. I was an enthusiastic new convert, hardly dry behind the ears, bringing my skeptical friends to hear Billy Graham speak in my huge college-football stadium. I blew off graduate school. Seeing people come to Christ was far more exciting. You could say, "Well, Paula sure drank the Kool-Aid," and you'd be right. Except it was more like I went to the cafeteria and drank every pitcher of every color Kool-Aid I could lay my hands on. I was *in*.

Of course, the reaction at home was not so enthusiastic. I remember discussing "my future" with my college-professor mother. She put it simple and straight: "Paula, you

---

35 Frank Sinatra, "My Way," *My Way* © 1969 Reprise Records.

are throwing your life away." For my mother, it was just that clear. She could see doors closing in ways I couldn't. And honestly, I didn't have a comeback.

I think I mumbled something about how, actually, I thought I had found life. If Jesus wasn't *life*, then what was? I remember sharing with her a verse that was pivotal for me at the time: "Whoever believes in Him will not be disappointed" (Romans 10:11, NASB). I was counting on that— not being disappointed.

My mother and I got nowhere in this conversation. Really, for the next thirty years, we got nowhere in that conversation.

So I continued to skip down the path that God had opened to me. And I was blissfully unaware that I had come to Christ in a unique period, one that would be chronicled later as a major revival era.[36] It was a beautiful thing—and a heady one.

To be a leader in such a movement, to touch the needs of the world with the message of Jesus Christ, is a wonderful aspiration. It's also a big vision that you can wrap your identity around with duct tape. I was sure I would become somebody—a real *somebody*—this way. Even my parents would see that I hadn't thrown my life away.

Maybe it sounds far-fetched to you that a person would latch onto something like "ministry" and get their actual self twisted into a pretzel around it. But this is the story of the human heart. We can attach ourselves to an infinite number

---

[36] In Norway, for example, students filled the state churches in the late '60s night after night, with candles and music and prayer. Actually, in every country that won World War II (the Allied powers), scores of students and young adults came to Christ between 1968 and 1972.

of things—sex, graduate degrees, a beautiful home, a person we love, you name it. We can transform almost anything into a ruler to measure our worth, or a place to stage our drama, or something we just cannot be without. To loosely quote John Calvin, the human heart is a doggone idol factory.[37]

Of course, Calvin had simply read the prophet Isaiah. Isaiah paints quite the graphic picture of how absurd it is to suppose anything inanimate or temporal can offer the utter transcendence we long for. Which is, to get to the heart of it, making it into God.

Here are Isaiah's words:

> All who fashion idols are nothing, and the things
> they delight in do not profit. . . . He feeds on ashes;
> a deluded heart has led him astray.[38]

We can turn anything into the seat of our deepest delight. Idolatry always has a delusional element to it—and that's what ministry was for me. Ministry, particularly in a revival era, is quite an effective thing to wrap yourself around. It can bring lots of applause. And it's *almost* Jesus.

Yes, it works wonderfully well . . . until the crowds go home. Even the original disciples noticed that was hugely deflating.[39] The exciting Christian enterprise becomes a journey of rather raw faithfulness when you realize the chairs still have to be set up for the next meeting. And again, next week.

---

37 John Calvin, *Institutes of the Christian Religion* (Basel, 1536), chap. 11.
38 Isaiah 44:20.
39 John 6:60-67.

Some of the folks who come will bring problems that five of you couldn't fix. You will no longer be a hero then, but a woman staring in the face of her own inadequacy.

Eventually, the emotional highs are fewer and further between. If you succumb to the temptation to measure your life in terms of ROI—return on investment—things don't add up. Often, there's not a lot of immediate profit. Not when the crowds go home.

You can imagine my surprise, then, when I started to hear faint echoes of the very disappointment I'd told my mother I was convinced God would save me from. Here I was, living my own little prosperity gospel, a utilitarian approach to faith that quietly but relentlessly asks, *What am I getting from this contract?* Oh, I was all in, as long as the adrenaline kept pumping. As long as I felt successful. But when the going got tough, I looked around for an easier route and louder applause.

You could say—and you'd be right—that I was trying to use God to become someone. It sounds bizarre, right? Trying to use God, when it appears for all the world that you are serving him. I was turning faith into a commodity. You don't know you are looking for a stroke to your ego until those strokes don't come much at all, and it's just you standing there with your hair in a mess and your dress in tatters in a room full of folks who aren't fans.

I read stories of people who hung out with Jesus as long as he supplied bread and miracles, and I could see my face among them. I could feel the pull to something snazzier than being the disciple of a God who ended up on a cross. The contrast between the utter thinness of my loyalty to Jesus and the thickness of his faithfulness to me was clear and painful.

One day, as I faced the reality that I couldn't conjure up an enthusiasm I didn't have, I started to pray. When I brought God my disappointment, he gave me the picture of a banquet table that stretched into the horizon. God showed me the corner and said to me, as clear as day, *Paula, I have kept your place at this table. It's waiting for you.* The words could just as easily have been spoken aloud. I was shocked spitless.

God had my number. He had known all along I was taking his love and making it a means to my own end. He knew I was feeding off the response of other people—not him. And he loved me enough to refuse to let me use him as a tool.

I felt like Peter, who expected a pink slip after his flakiness became known. Wouldn't you have pulled Jesus aside and said, "Look, you can find somebody better than *Peter*"? And I knew well that I stood in Peter's shoes. By all rights, I should have been sent packing. And here was Jesus, instead, inviting me to take a place at a table already prepared—feeding me, really, with himself.

It is said that the love of God *always* comes as a surprise. I think there's real truth to that. The enterprise of Christianity was never going to sustain me. And God knew that all along. Our search for identity and meaning can only be satisfied in him. Only his love will ever prove enough.

So this was the landscape of my life in which I came to recognize that sinfulness lies not on the surface but at the core of my being. Facing the fallenness of the world must include facing the fallenness of *what is* in me. It becomes a primary place where I meet God—and discover grace that opens a door to *what can be*. The Good News of the gospel is that I am not forever stuck.

There is so much mercy in being able to own the darkness of your own heart. You'd think you would be stuck forever in hopeless despair. But a door opens as it did for the woman of the city, and against all odds, Jesus is there, offering you kind words and his embrace.

Understanding who you are in this *what is* allows a wild freedom to invade your life. This God who won't be used by you or me, who insists that he is actually GOD, dissolves our little measuring stick of performance and lets us have a small part in the Kingdom he is building. On many occasions, that includes the equivalent of setting up the chairs. But you don't have to become *somebody*. You are the somebody Jesus loves. *Already.* And that does prove to be quite enough.

In the church that my husband and I attend, at one point during the service, we as a congregation get down on our knees to quietly confess our sin. It's helped me so much to have my body led through the paces of repentance every week. I own my wayward heart, receive God's embrace, and stand up to sing. This is the natural exercise of the soul, the actual rhythm that's meant to mark our lives all the time.

What I find is that the more I tell the truth about who I am, the clearer I hear the mercy of God. And the more I long to follow him well.

In this arena of naming personal sin, we have to step over a culture quite adverse to that. Naming sin can sound harsh. A bit judgmental, even. Like having your own internal Pharisee jab you in the side: *I know what sort of woman you are.* Maybe for half your life you've had somebody calling out your deficiencies and you are sick of that. I have a friend who insists that when it comes to personal sin, she just doesn't think in those categories anymore—in the same way she doesn't go down dark alleys where a bully might beat her up.

I hope you can hear something profoundly different in what Connally and I are describing.

When Connally's friend has the nerve (!) to tell her that she oozes arrogance and Connally realizes, *Wow, on some level, that's me,* her sin takes a known shape. She can feel the impact on others—the cost they pay. And she is ten steps closer to chains breaking inside of her.

It's the same for me. When I acknowledge the dark side of my good girl who has the audacity to try to enlist God in her *somebody* project, I am dancing in the street. I no longer have to live under her tyranny.

Peace comes with the truth. The chunks of us that are chronically prone to dethrone God and put ourselves in his place? They're real and relentless. Apart from Jesus' rescue, our bent would shut us out from God's presence, for keeps. But Jesus is real and relentless too. That's why looking at all this reality in the eye and naming it as such is simply, flat-out freedom.

Facing our personal sin also helps us confront the reality of a world where evil is at work. We are a little less tempted to call evil *good*—or to call good *evil*—which Isaiah says is the mark of decadence, both personal and cultural. It takes courage to face the wrong in a world that so actively chooses rebellion against God, be it through systemic racism, disregard for life, or self-centered choices. Willingness to name our own sin makes us better able to humbly call things as they are—because we see the seeds of the same in our very own selves.

All of this is what the Bible calls *the path of life*. God promised to lead us down this path.[40] We get to go home. And we are kicking up our heels all the way. Ongoing acknowledgment of sin and the need for repentance is what brings life—more and more life.

So, yes, we are living in a day that begs us to wallpaper over our flaws and foibles with happy talk. But we don't just have a friend in Jesus. We have a God who came in search of us. He follows us down a dark alley, names the dirt we are covered with, and cleans us up. He sets a table before us and feeds us with himself.

---

[40] Psalm 16:11.

Reflections
on

NAKED, AFRAID, AND NOT SO NICE

1. There is great freedom in being able to name and own personal
    sin. Connally wrote about her struggle with racism and
    privilege. Paula talked about the idolatry of using anything as
    a means of identity, a way to be "somebody." Which of those
    stories do you most identify with? Why?

2. What inhibits you from naming the darkness in your heart in
    specific ways? In what ways might that darkness be a strange
    sort of saving grace?

3. The Bible leads us to actually name our hang-ups, shortcomings,
    and besetting sins—to move from the general to the specific.
    It's part of overcoming and breaking free. Colossians 3:5-9 is
    a classic list of the kinds of sin we all struggle with. Read this
    passage. What of these do you identify most with. Why?

4. Connally shared the story of the "woman of the city" who burst
    into a group of pious men so she could encounter this Jesus
    for herself. Tune into the personal words that Jesus spoke
    about this woman (Luke 7:44-50). What strikes you most about
    this passage?

5. Connally wrote about the release and freedom that come from experiencing the embrace of God in the place we may least hope for it—*our own sin*. When have you experienced a taste of that? How has that affected your life and experience of God?

6. The apostle John wrote the oft-quoted words that when we confess our sin, God is faithful and just not only to forgive us—but to cleanse us from that sin and to allow us to walk in the light again with him.[41] What has been one experience or season in your life when you've known the power of being forgiven and set free?

7. After you've read this chapter, how does the ongoing acknowledgment of sin and the need for repentance look different to you?

---

[41] 1 John 1:9.

What Can Be

REDEMPTION

WE HAVE LINGERED A BIT on the *what is* of a fallen world. But this lingering is important. To journey well, a traveler needs to know not just a region's glory spots but also something of the tough terrain through which she will travel. That preparation will keep her going, even when the ground gets barren or the roads too twisty.

The hard realities you encounter along the way are far from the whole story. They are simply the dark shadows against which the contrasting Good News of Jesus radiates all the more brightly, in a sort of divine chiaroscuro. For there is something bigger than *what is*. There is another chapter in God's big Story. There is something more that really *can be*. This is called *redemption*.

In the midst of fallenness—within our world and very selves—the light of Christ breaks through the darkness. His coming changes everything. His resurrection makes possible redemption that we can see and experience in the present—and complete restoration to come. But we have to follow him as we move forward, believing that we will see the goodness of the Lord "in the land of the living."

The question as we journey becomes: *What story of redemption is God writing in and through my life?*

CHAPTER 4

THE STARTING POINT

What Redemption Looks Like

You are stuck in a dark tunnel. It's nearly impossible to get your bearings. Where's up? Where's down? Are there birds singing somewhere outside?

But wait. A pinprick of light pierces the sea of blackness. You're pretty sure you saw it. As you stare in that direction, the light expands. You get up and walk toward the light. Your hands and feet take shape. You are actually leaving this tunnel. It's a new world on the other side—or maybe it's the old world you are seeing with new eyes. You're not quite sure.

Possibilities are opening up. New opportunities that won't be lost now. Promises that can be kept. You hear the sound of chains breaking; they pile up around your feet.

It's a whole new lightness of being. And yes, the song of birds fills the air.

The possibility of seeing redemption in your life is a lot like stepping out of the dark and realizing you aren't exactly home—indeed, you're in a new country of some sort.

Redemption as we know it in Jesus Christ is a miracle unique to the gospel. It does not deny or eliminate all traces of *what is*. It's not based on pretending. Rather, redemption has a way of swallowing up the sting of the Fall and opening us to a new and eternal life that begins now.

You are watching the goodness of God unfold—perhaps in ways you could not have anticipated—in your present life.

Remember the woman of the city in the last chapter? Jesus told her to "go in peace." But if you were her, wouldn't you be asking the next question—*Where exactly do I go?*

Redemption leads you forward. And if you'll let it, redemption will infuse your soul and connect you far more deeply to the goodness of God. How do you follow the threads of redemption in your life so you step into as much of God's goodness as is possible?

EYES OF FAITH

Connally

Sometime in my early thirties, on a work trip to Colorado, I listened to a woman named Ruth Myers as she spoke to a few of us organizational newcomers. She was probably forty years my senior, and she was sharing about her life, about the death of her first husband, and about what knowing Jesus Christ had looked like for her over many years. Besides those general points, I don't remember much of what she said.

But I remember looking in her eyes.

Her eyes were like pools, blue-gray with age and warm with a light that hinted at interior fire. Think of coals that have burned long enough to deeply settle in—radiant, glowing, inviting.

I was mesmerized. I could not stop looking at her. It was as if her faith and Jesus' love were pouring out of her eyes.

Repeatedly, her gaze met mine. My glance danced around. I felt a bit scared that my sputtering, birthday-candle-sized faith would reveal its paltry self. But I longed to keep staring, as if in so doing, I could absorb something of the very certain hope that bubbled up in her.

After the meeting, she and I spoke briefly, and she kindly invited me to contact her anytime. But it wasn't advice or even a listening ear that I was after. It wasn't about an exchange of words. I simply longed to look at her eyes.

Those eyes have stayed with me. I think in many ways, they lit something in me. In one sense, hers were, quite simply, the eyes of Jesus. She gazed into me with a deep knowledge that cut through my defenses and poured out God's radiant love.

But there was something else as well—as if a spark of faith jumped across a ravine and caught my dried-up hope on fire. From what she'd shared, her life had sometimes been breathtakingly hard. Those eyes, though, still glistened. Beautifully.

The meetings in Colorado took ten days. Eighteen years later, I have only the vaguest recollection of what they were about. But one takeaway from that time has never left me:

Because I am deeply seen and loved by the living God, I can go the distance and still end up with eyes that dance, bringing light to others. And what more, I have come to realize, could a person really want?

GOODNESS IN THE LAND OF THE LIVING

One sunny Friday afternoon when Paula and I were catching up on the phone, she asked me about the specific ways I'd tasted the goodness of Jesus' redemption in my life. Her question made me pause. When your faith is young and fresh, the answer to such a question can seem obvious: *Oh! Knowing Jesus Christ has brought me new energy, new friends, new hope!* Oftentimes, too, there are unquestionably direct and personal answers to prayer. *I prayed my uncle would stop smoking, and three weeks later, he quit. I asked for a job, and would you believe I got an offer while I was on an escalator?* Honestly, it seems like if you are new to faith in Jesus, the starting point is just to stick your toes in the water and discover what can be: Waves divinely part, and paths emerge out of nowhere!

After you've journeyed with Jesus for a while, however, you've probably experienced some hard hits. In the midst of that, it can take guts to keep looking with earnest expectation for the goodness of *what can be* with Jesus. Honestly, sometimes we must choose to plunge by faith through the darkness of our own valleys to seek out the goodness that the psalmist says will follow us all the days of our lives.[42] This can be scary,

---

[42] Psalm 23:6.

but it is worth the risk because the goodness of our Redeemer is really there. Even the holes in our souls can be portals to the goodness of his heart.[43]

Whether a follower of Jesus is wet behind the ears or a seasoned, salty saint, the goodness of redemption can take a hundred different forms. When it's fleshed out in real lives, sometimes goodness looks like amazing changes in circumstances. My brother and sister-in-law, who lived in the Middle East for more than twenty-five years, were forever telling tales of the miraculous: Divine deliverance in dangerous situations (like the last-minute provision of a military helicopter to help them escape a suddenly erupting war). Visions of Jesus coming in the night to those who'd never heard about him. Money arriving in the right amount at the right time to pay the seemingly unpayable bill. A careening car brought to a mysterious halt six inches before crashing into their family's minivan.

But when I bring my gaze home, honestly appraising my own journey, the goodness of redemption mostly has looked like God slowly forming me to walk more closely with him, to be more like him. The goodness of *what can be* always shows up as God's tenacious and loving commitment to see us *fathered, freed,* and *fruitful.*[44]

What can be through Jesus' redemption is an experience of goodness that is part echo of the Garden and part foretaste

---

43 The presence of God's goodness does not preclude some of us going through a dark night of the soul when God seems absent, his goodness inaccessible.

44 My friend, Susan Simpson, coled a ministry in Russia for many years. *Fathered, freed,* and *fruitful* were the concepts around which she, her husband, and her teammates sought to form this emerging community of new believers. I have found these ideas very helpful when thinking about my own journey and those of others around me.

of our promised future. Even with ample fallenness tangling up this world, we can receive something substantive of the deep security and love we once had and will one day fully know with the Father. We can be set free from the compelling need to hide behind fig leaves even as we're clothed with Jesus' fresh and righteous robes. And once again, we can taste the joy of bearing good, eternally valuable fruit in the world around us.

Fathered

In Russia, like in many places and in many people's lives, fatherhood does not always look like loving strength seeking the well-being of a child. My friend Susan lived in Russia for more than fifteen years, where she was deeply involved in the lives of an emerging multigenerational community of faith. She explained to me that for her Russian friends, *father* sometimes had such negative connotations that *our Father in heaven* was hard to say. Many people there—and increasingly here in the States as well—connect *father* to abuse, abandonment, or a seemingly innocuous yet devastating barely-there-ness.

Knowing each of us has a unique experience—sometimes positive, sometimes negative, often somewhere in between—with a human dad, I want to gently press back into this word that was so important to Jesus: *Father.* Jesus used this name for God 120 times in the Gospel of John—120 times in twenty-one chapters. This name, and the relationship it speaks to, mattered to Jesus.

Even a quick look at the word *Father* in the book of John

reveals the profound connectedness between Jesus and his Father. This Father gives to his Son, works with his Son, shows himself to his Son. He shares honor with his Son, grants life to his Son, and calls his Son *beloved*.[45] Meanwhile, down on dusty planet Earth, the Son knows he is from his Father, knows his Father is at his side, and does what he somehow, mysteriously, sees his Father doing. The Son pours out his longings to his Father, entrusting his life, death, and resurrection to his Father's hands.

Can you feel the profoundly intimate connection between the two? Can you imagine being that tightly tied to that good of a Father? It's as if Jesus' very sense of self is integrally woven into his Father. Who is Jesus? He is the Son of his Father. See the Son? You've seen his Dad.

In an era where many of us feel like our sense of identity is up for grabs, a fluid thing vaguely sourced by some self-selected combination of desires, what might it be like to discover a sense of self fueled by our relationship to a loving Father? What might shift in us if we discovered we were defined less by *what we desire* than by *Who desires us*?

This, I believe, is what it is to be fathered. It's to discover inside yourself—in that place where all your presuppositions and emotions about life linger—that because Jesus has made it possible, the God of the universe gives to you, works with you, shows himself to you. He shares honor with you, grants life to you, and calls you his beloved. And as his daughter, you grow to know that you're created by your Father, who is

---

45 Matthew 3:17.

at your side, showing you the work he has for you. You get to pour out your longings to him, entrusting your life, death, and ultimate resurrection to him.

As we grow in this deep knowledge of our Father (fed by the Scriptures, the Spirit, corporate worship, and other believers), like Jesus, we can grow in our capacity to recognize his voice. For me, his has been the voice that so often says, *I am with you, keep going*—or, conversely, *You know you need to let this go, Connally.*

When I was deciding to move back to my hometown, his was the voice that repeatedly said, *Pursue this; pursue Charlottesville.* When I was faced with a real-estate contract "gone bad," his was the voice that kept saying, *Though your own father is gone, I will bring you the human help you need.*

Even when I was crying out one Memorial Day weekend, *Why don't I have a family with whom to make and eat ice cream?*, his was the voice that responded, *I delight in you; I'm crazy about you; you are mine.* That wasn't the answer I was hoping for, but his words landed deep inside me, calming my frantic heart.

At the core of being divinely fathered, we encounter the one who brings us his intimate strength, wisdom, and even atta-girls, promising to be with us always. This does *not* make life's problems disappear. But as we become women grounded and defined by our Father's love, we discover what it is to keep growing up, with twinkles still in our eyes. Whether or not our own fathers have shown up well, we get to walk with our Father in new gardens of his making. And this is a very good thing.

Freed

With the loving strength of our Father ever more real in our lives, we also can discover deeper tastes of freedom. Freedom is rarely a linear process, of course. But buttressed by the One Who Is There, we are increasingly set free from ugly powers in our lives. The hooks of guilt, shame, and a host of other uglies are slowly unhitched from our hearts—sometimes with repeatedly tough tugs but always by gentle hands. God's goodness shines as he removes from us the burdensome need for fig leaves, clothing us in his fresh and righteous robes.

FROM GUILT AND UNFORGIVENESS

I am seventeen, watching this super-cool college student, Eddie, hold up a glass of water. He drops a drop or two of red food coloring into the glass. The water takes on a faint pink tint. "This," he says, "is like our sin. Even a few drops taint all of who we are."

Nodding up and down, I know he's right. It makes sense, too, when someone adds, "Yeah, and Jesus' blood is like bleach, which takes out all the stain." It's a homespun analogy, but it resonates with me. I know in me resides a wanna-be queen, hungry for the throne, even if it means knocking God off his. And I know I'm not powerful enough to put her in her place.

It's a crazy joy, then, to realize that my guilt for such

an attitude—and all its related practices—is taken care of. When I shake off the dark enchantments of my mind and acknowledge I'm *not queen* (which is another way of saying "I repent"), Jesus frees up my insecure self to live into her proper place with the Father. This is why I love the confession part of the worship service in my church. Naming specific sins and laying them before Jesus each week is like pulling burrs off my socks after a hike. Or taking the pebbles out of my boots. I lay down those burrs, those pebbles, and I'm reminded once again of God's forgiveness. My conscience clear, I'm freed to walk forward—humbly owning for my missteps with others and making amends where needed.

Equally good, though, is the freedom *to forgive* some of those very same others.

I remember picking up a photo once of a person who had hurt me—intentionally or not, I'll never know. Conversation alone had never been enough to solve the breach. But I knew when I looked at that picture that somehow I was still chained to this person. (You know that you are still chained when you find yourself giving mental speeches to a picture.)

At that point, I put the picture down, and for the umpteenth time in my life, I pulled out what I've fondly come to label my "forgiveness worksheets." Slowly but surely, I made my way through these preset words. At the end, I was able to squeak out as I'd done before in different situations: "Lord, I give up the right to be judge, jury, and prosecuting attorney in these matters. This person now answers to you, not me." Envisioning Jesus' shed blood spilling down and balancing the scales of injustice between this person and me, I forgave.

I could almost hear the chains between us break and fall.

"Forgive as the Lord forgave you."[46] This is the admonition of Scripture, over and over again. It's what being Jesus-like looks like. But it's also this quiet invitation to freedom. Imagine just for a moment the scads of wounding words and head-spinning hits you've gathered in your years. What might it feel like to forgive? Can you picture that other person's stuff—right next to *your* stuff—nailed to the cross?

Forgiveness is sometimes a onetime thing; sometimes it has to be repeated, over and over again, as layers of hurt are peeled away. But whether it takes one or seventy-seven times, the amazing thing is, forgiveness is possible.[47] Forgiven ourselves, we are empowered to let others off the hook on which they might very well deserve to hang. And as we make our way along this path, we just might discover that our shoulders relax, our lungs fill, and one hundred pounds of weight lift off us. Past wrongs—yours, mine, or ours—no longer have to haunt our imaginations or shackle our feet. I can look at that picture and genuinely want this friend's well-being, even as I'm freed to turn my attention in new directions.

FROM SHAME

Have you ever felt ashamed? Do you know that ugly prospect of being seen through the lens of "less than"? Has your vague

---

46 Colossians 3:13, NIV.
47 Matthew 18:21-22.

sense of your own unworthiness or dishonor left you feeling naked, afraid, and wanting to hide? This is called shame.

A family friend innocently asks me about my real-estate contract gone bad. Knowing I lack the verbal skills of a litigator, I start scrambling in a weird frenzy to make sure this friend knows I wasn't foolish in the transaction.

I tell a story to a small group of women, revealing a place of sexual struggle in my life, and I read my listeners' faces. Real or imagined, their perceived disapproval triggers my heart racing, heat flashing through me.

A new hairstylist asks me about my husband and children. When I tell her I've always been single and childless, her silence screams to me, "Misfit!" and I suddenly feel defensive. I want to run and take cover.

David, that Israelite king who lived a thousand years before Jesus was born, understood this need for cover. A strong, faithful, adulterating, honest, murderous, God-seeking mixed bag of a great man knew that God not only covered David's sin but could protect him from the reproach of others, from wagging tongues, from danger. David knew what it was to want to run and hide. But repeatedly—as he learned to run toward and hide in his heavenly Father—he discovered what it was to find himself safely covered.

Sometime, you might study how David uses that word *cover* in his poems, recorded in the biblical book of Psalms.[48] His situations were, of course, unusually dire. Most of us aren't kings facing fickle masses or angry political enemies.

---

[48] Psalm 27:5, 31:20.

But as I've tried to put David's words into practice, turning to our Father for cover when shame attacks me, I've found that I can slow down and breathe.

"Cover me, Lord," I've learned to whisper.

I've got you covered with my fresh and righteous robes, he reminds me.

"Oh yes . . . sorry. I forgot. But thank you."

Inevitably, this reminder settles me on the inside. I find myself replying to that hair stylist, "Yep, sometimes it can be socially awkward to be single and childless. But the truth is, I'm actually okay—more than okay, come to think of it."

In the warmth of his cover, the *misfit* label melts away. The lie has no more power over me. And I walk away that afternoon, emboldened, with really great-looking hair.

Fruitful

The word *fruitful* has always pulled me in. One Christmas, somebody gave our family a subscription to the Fruit of the Month Club, and every month for the next twelve, some new cardboard box of fruit would arrive. I remember discovering kiwis; those fuzzy, green, and juicy fruits, replete with tiny black seeds, were like a passport to another land, hinting at the sweetness we forever long for. Oh, and there was a box of amazing peaches. Even now, peach juice running down my wrist can whisper of a lost childhood luxury: summer, sunshine, and timelessly lingering over one of God's tastiest gifts.

It makes great sense to me that God uses the metaphor of fruit again and again to describe what we are to bring into this world. Increasingly fathered, we are freed to cultivate tangible tastes of eternity. In Genesis, God called the animals to be fruitful and multiply.[49] He called our first parents (and now us) to do the same.[50] Oftentimes, this looks like having babies, reproducing image bearers. But it also means cultivating whatever gifts or talents we've been given to bear all kinds of other fruit—like a farmer planting a sea of wheat, a builder building bridges, a painter bringing life to a canvas, a hostess offering a beautiful meal.

Actually, one of my biggest questions as an increasingly fathered-and-freed but still single woman has been, *Where does a childless woman's love land, really? What does it look like to be lovingly fruitful when I'm seemingly a solo act?* To my unceasing shock, honestly, I've discovered that my love has landed and borne its own fruit. Paths have opened for me to come alongside a host of children—nieces, nephews, godchildren, and others—cheering, listening, and offering input that needs to come from a nonparent. And in my relationships with a variety of others—through direct-ministry contexts and informally—I've been able to plant seeds of faith, hope, and love. I've also been able to cultivate conversations around race and ethnicity in my small circles, breaking up some of the hard ground that typically hinders progress in conversations about these topics.

Our fruitfulness, though, goes far beyond our own stories. In the life of faith, we also get to participate in multiplying the Good News about Jesus Christ in others' lives. Joined to him, mysteriously we can serve as cocreators in others'

---

49 Genesis 1:22.
50 Genesis 1:28.

new or deepening faith. Whether we are listening and asking good questions, telling the truth about how we've seen God be real in our lives, or simply pointing to what the Scriptures say about him, we plant hope that can grow in others' hearts. I've never found a formula to make this so, but somehow the gospel manages to keep flowing through us—in spite of and sometimes through our very cracks—into others' lives.

Are you starting to get the idea? Because we are fathered and freed, the pathways to our fruitfulness are never-ending, as varied as our individual lives. But always, as we turn and return—over the days, months, and years—to *what can be* with Jesus, we taste his goodness. This is goodness, the psalmist confidently reminds us, that we get to see in the land of the living.[51] The journey might come with hits harder than we think we can endure, but fathered, freed, and fruitful, we can continue, radiant with living proof of the goodness of Jesus' redemption: eyes that still dance with earnest expectation.

THE ACT OF TURNING TO GOD

Paula

Living in the world of redemption, of *what can be*, means walking toward the light. And even when the darkness closes around you, as it sometimes does, you hold on to the light you remember . . . until you can see straight again.

Living in *what can be* is really about the many ways we

---

[51] Psalm 27:13.

simply turn to God. In an acknowledgment of his presence in all things. In repentance for our unbelief. With a willingness to forgive and be forgiven. In the midst of our shame and guilt.

We step a little deeper, in each turning, into the reality that we do have a Father and we are no-joke freed from stuff that would keep us pinned to the wall. Beauty and life are emerging from ashes.

We can experience this *what can be* of God in our lives through the simple, invisible act of turning to God in the moment. When we turn to God in the mundane stuff of our lives—and the brutally hard places as well—the literal cosmos cracks open, just a tiny tear. Perhaps that's why prayer is more powerful than it appears. Through that tear we step, little by little, into another piece of the redemption that Christ won for us by his cross and resurrection.

In redemption, God carries us along this "path of life" described so often in Scripture, where doors open, wounds get more healed, courage is given—really, where the glory of God shows up in quiet but very real ways.

In fact, if you talk with someone who has seen God's power and faithfulness over many years, you'll hear a story of someone who has simply come back to the well and taken another drink. Over and over. On some level, it's as simple as the prescription that David gave in his psalm: "My soul clings to you; your right hand upholds me."[52]

That is the rub, though, isn't it? It's just not our natural inclination to turn to God. At least it's not mine, for sure.

---

[52] Psalm 63:8.

No, I'm inclined to keep the motor humming, pour on more activity, go to the mall. Paint furniture or pay bills. Oh, it's an incredible privilege to do life with God, that I know. And I deeply believe we can be fathered, freed, and fruitful. I really do. It's just that in the day in, day out of regular life, the dialogue breaks down. I pick up my phone as soon as it pings, but this God who calls out to me in a hundred ways (most notably through his Word)? *That* I dial back to a faint whisper.

Every heart comes up to this fork in the road, many times. Life bruises you—and you are faced again with the choice: Are you going to move toward God and other people, or are you going to tunnel inward to that false-but-safe isolation with which we are all so terribly familiar?

So in those places in your life where you are honestly more inclined to run in every direction *but God*, I want to recommend to you a coach.

I discovered this guy during the ups and downs of infertility in our family, in a season when I was all prayed out. At some point in the world of earnest prayer, we become distinctly aware that we have run up against the word *no*. Like, really, *no*. Not going to happen. (And I had hit that wall.)

I was incredibly tempted just to let silence reign between God and me. I didn't want to turn toward the God who, I felt, had caused the actual pain. How could I draw comfort from the God who had wounded me? (Big question, that.)

I've learned through years of listening to others—and listening to my own life—that right at this juncture, we are prone to run away. Like, *I'll get back to God when I'm in better shape and am more confident in him.* Much as we might put on lipstick before we walk into a room of people, we want to pretty ourselves up before we bare our insides to the God who can see them anyway.

"God," I said, "I need someone else's words to pray here." And then immediately, a thought came to me: *What are the worst words in Scripture?*

That's when I was introduced to a cranky old prophet I didn't know much about. He became a friend and a guide, and when I get to heaven, I am going to hug his neck, big-time. He's gotten a bad rap through the years because, as I say, he's a bit cranky (and with good reason). But oh, he's been there. He's lived in the dark places that you and I only visit on occasion.

Moment by moment, for almost a month, I sat with Jeremiah, who sat with God. I let him do the talking. I read the same passage out of the third chapter of Lamentations every morning, until I almost knew it by heart.

> You seem to me a bear lying in wait, ready to get me.
> You have walled me in, and I am trapped. You've
> made my chains heavy. My endurance is nearly
> gone—and so is my hope.[53]

I was startled by the honesty in Jeremiah's words. This was *God* he was talking to. Here was this man who had been thrown into a pit by his equivalent of "other believers"— other practicing Jewish leaders—and he felt betrayed by the

---

[53] Lamentations 3:10-11, author's paraphrase.

living God. His words mirror what we think in our worst moments of pain and distortion—when it feels like we've been left by the side of the road somewhere and nothing good will ever happen again.

Except that we know better. Somewhere in our heads, we know better. But we can't quite access what we know.

So there I was each morning, watching Jeremiah do the unthinkable. *He was wrestling with his distortions of God—with God.* The living God was not striking him dead, or sending him away in shame, but holding him close until he could see reality again.

How do I know this? Because if you listen closely, you can hear a giant exhale in his conversation with God. When Jeremiah has spent himself, he stops and breathes deep the air of mercy. *Oh, yes,* I can almost imagine him saying to himself, *I remember.*

> The steadfast love of the LORD never ceases;
>   his mercies never come to an end;
> they are new every morning;
>   great is your faithfulness.[54]

Some of the most-loved words of Scripture are Jeremiah's. They are the words of a man who was in an awful place and washed up on the shore of trust, who was anchored once again by remembering that the Lord is especially good to those who wait for him.[55]

---

[54] Lamentations 3:22-23.
[55] Lamentations 3:25. (Also see Psalm 37:9; Isaiah 30:18; 49:23; 64:4; and Hebrews 9:28).

As for Jeremiah, so it began being for me. Every morning, his words squeezed the toxicity out of my soul just a bit more. I could see clearly again. *What I'm counting on here is not the dream—it's the faithfulness of God.*

I'm grateful for this man who became my coach in a rough time. He showed me that if I would simply turn to God without my lipstick, risking that he's actually good, God would meet me. His redemption can take a hundred forms—and it may be quite a while in coming. Sometimes we see only faint hints. Occasionally, it's as concrete as the sound of a little girl's laughter in the next room and a song she sings to herself: "We sing hallelujah, the Lamb has overcome."[56]

BUT LIFE IS JUST SO ORDINARY

Not all turning to God is this difficult of a journey through silence and distance. Not by a long shot. We attach to God—through whom all redemption comes—something like we attached, at least ideally, to the first human in our lives: our mothers. We got hungry, and they gave us milk. We brought them daisies and they smiled at the wonder and beauty. We learned there was someone there to share moments of every sort.

The starting point of all that's possible—the actual *what can be* of your life—unfolds out of similar small encounters with God. Those moments might contain grief or shame or fear. But they might just as easily look like the little Motown

---

[56] Kari Jobe, "Forever," *Majestic* © 2014 Sparrow.

jig I do when a sudden glimpse of the Blue Ridge Mountains triggers joy and wonder, and I just cannot help but say, "Thank-you, Jesus. You are more beautiful than even these mountains."

Turning to God covers a wide landscape of experience: those brutally hard times in your life—like the one that Jeremiah coached me through—and the exceedingly everyday. Maybe the everyday kinds are the easiest to miss.

When I think of mundane times, I recall a recent moment in a Hallmark store, where I went to buy Christmas paper. I don't usually buy Christmas paper there because it's too nice to be torn to shreds. But you get desperate, right?

So there I was, inspecting every roll of Christmas paper they have because it's funky and nothing looks like traditional Christmas. And for some reason, all of that strikes a nerve. There's too much change happening in my life as it is. My grandchildren are growing up, my body is slowing down, and I hardly recognize the world I'm in. I'm in no mood for ridiculously expensive blue-and-orange Christmas paper that's going to end up in a pile on the floor.

I feel the need to share a bit of my angst with the clerk as I check out: "Could you pass on to the designers in New York that, even in the South, we know Santa Claus didn't dress in blue rectangles and triangles—not originally, anyway?"

Those are the moments when I know I need to take a deep breath. I heard my own harried voice. I was back in that internally isolated place, where everything is resting on my shoulders. That state of frazzle tells me it's past time to turn to God.

So that night, as I reviewed the day, I reviewed some familiar Bible verses. As I drifted off to sleep, I let the words rain down on me: "The LORD is my light and my salvation; whom shall I fear? The LORD is the defense of my life; whom shall I dread?"[57]

I could breathe again. *Nothing that matters, Paula, has changed.* Sometimes, the first edge of redemption is the calm that puts things in perspective so you can walk forward in a life where you can rarely dictate the terms.

In God, there are infinite possibilities. As the lyrics of one of Christa Wells's songs puts it, he is "a tree always in bloom." This triune God is "a hall of endless rooms."[58] The power of his death and resurrection bleeds into your present moment: As you turn to him, he shares his life with you.

It's his power, then, that lets you risk adopting a child. Or helps you walk into a room of strangers when you are unsure of what you'll say. Or comforts you as you realize the limitations of the man you just married. Or gives you the courage to say no even when your friend's feelings will be hurt if you do.

It's his power that enables us to walk forward—fathered, freed, and fruitful. We are not stuck in the hard, cold reality of *what is*. There is always more to your story because there's always a Larger Story. When you least expect it, doors open to possibilities of *what can be*. And some of them are better than you would even dare to dream.

---

57 Psalm 27:1, NASB.
58 Christa Wells, "Everything Moves but You," *How Emptiness Sings* © 2011 Kiss Me Not Publishing.

Reflections
on
THE STARTING POINT

1. As you consider the reality of the redemption that Jesus brings, whose eyes (or smile, words, or way in this world) have reflected the alluring goodness and power of Jesus' redemption to you? What has been particularly powerful about this person or your experience with him or her?

2. Read Psalm 27. This is a song of King David, who—in spite of life's fearful troubles—was able to declare that he would "see the goodness of the LORD in the land of the living."[59] How do you respond to David's declaration? Where have you seen this goodness of the Lord in your own life? In what places in your life does his goodness seem distant or inaccessible? What might it mean for you to ask and look for his goodness in those very difficult or chaotic places?

3. When you read about God being our Father, what comes to mind for you? How has your experience with your own father (for good, for ill, or somewhere in between) shaped your understanding of God as Father? How might you grow in your

---

59 Psalm 27:13, NIV.

personal knowledge of the loving-kindness of your heavenly Father? For example, you might look up the references to God as Father in the book of John and note what you discover. Or you might slowly pray through the Lord's Prayer (Matthew 6:9-13) for a week, noting each day what the prayer itself reveals about who our Father is. Whatever you do, ask him to make his loving-kindness ever more real to you and look for his answer.

4. Consider the freedom from guilt that comes through forgiveness—the forgiveness we receive and the forgiveness we can offer. Consider, too, the freedom from shame that comes from a recognition that we are covered and honored by the Lord. In what areas of your life have you discovered the freedom of forgiveness (receiving it or giving it)? In what areas of your life have you been set free from shame? In light of your journey so far, what freedom do you need as you turn your attention to the future?

5. The fruit of redemption in our own lives (and that which spills over into the lives of others) can take hundreds of forms. What "fruitfulness" have you seen multiplied in or through your life thus far? Put differently, where have your gifts and talents borne life? What has been sweet to you about this fruitbearing? What other fruit do you dream of bearing?

6. The journey of redemption includes returning again and again to the Lord, like returning to a well for a drink. When you hear this, how do you respond? What might this repeated returning look like in the context of your current, ordinary life? What might it take for this to become a regular and even joyful practice in your life going forward?

CHAPTER 5

SEEING REDEMPTION IN INTERIOR SPACES

Wound, Lie, Choices, Truth

Paula

Something supernatural happens in the ordinary act of turning to God. The Holy One of Israel hears you, and his Spirit translates your simplest plea. You are tapping into the very power that raised Jesus Christ from the dead. So it's bigger than it looks.

Here's one thing I find amazing about the gospel: The Spirit of God doesn't just give you hope for your exterior world—he reshapes your interior space. Honestly, it can feel like small explosions of redemption. And from this quiet rearranging of your internal furniture, so to speak, you move into life in ways you could not have remotely touched on your own.

As a Christian and a therapist, I'm pretty familiar with

"internal spaces," my own and other people's. I have a healthy appreciation for what good counseling offered me at a critical point in my life. I'm grateful I get to offer that help to others.

But there was a season in my experience when I was overly enamored with psychology and Jungian thought, as though it might offer some "secret truth" that could unlock your life. It wouldn't save your soul, exactly; that I knew. But plumbing the depths of your psyche could yield hidden treasure, new freedoms. Something like deep inner peace. It's really a Gnostic notion that finding one's true self is the key to life.[60] *Is there something missing in the gospel itself?* I wondered.

Then I began to work with actual people on the gritty stuff we all face. I began to confront my own gritty stuff. *And it was psychology that was not enough.* Slowly, I realized that without the language of sin and repentance and redemption—without the transcendent reality of this God who came—you just couldn't "get at" the stuck places of the soul. Not mine or anyone else's.

As I worked with person after person, the gospel hit me all over again—this time with genuine awe. This God who took on our form and died our death, who feeds us in the ongoing sacrament of his body and nourishes our inmost being through prayer and the care of others who bear his name—what can compare? That you can stand before him without shame, forgiven. Loved. This is not the stuff of dry theology. It's a flat-out miracle.

---

60 This "secret truth" thing is always the promise of Gnosticism, an ancient heresy that has plagued the church in different forms in every generation, especially ours. Gnosticism is a religious hyperindividualism that blurs the lines between the God out there, who made himself known in Christ, and the god within, the disembodied self.

FOUR WORDS

This path to this interior change isn't just theoretical, something that sounds nice. In fact, you can use highly practical handles, an intentional process, to invite the work of God's Spirit into your life. Over time, you'll actually see things change. *What can be*—what redemption looks like in your interior world—becomes quite real.

This process follows four meaningful words: *wound, lie, choices, truth*. I think you could excavate any piece of redemptive change in your life and find that these words resonate:

- the *wound* you encountered,
- the *lie* you believed,
- the *choices* you made,
- and the *truth* God wants you to embrace.

As you follow this process, I hope you can see how God's Spirit actually uses the pain of life to uproot and expose the lies that keep you in bondage—and how in that fresh, upturned soil, God plants reality. Truth. Something so solid that you return, again and again, and build out from there, like God himself is laying new claim to the life you were always meant to live. I think of this as the embodiment of C. S. Lewis's wonderful words, paraphrased—that when we are wholly God's, we will be more ourselves than ever before.[61]

---

[61] A statement most thoroughly covered in Lewis's classic work *Mere Christianity*: "The more we get what we now call 'ourselves' out of the way and let Him take us over, the more truly ourselves we become"; *The Complete C. S. Lewis Signature Classics* (New York: HarperSanFrancisco, 2002), 118.

The Wound

As is often said, the personal is universal, meaning that when any of us speak of longing and sin and the search for love, we are pretty much telling the same stories. So I offer my story in the humility of realizing it represents much of the human dilemma we call life. My particular story begins with my mother and me.

I wish you had known this woman. She came from a place so deep in the Virginia mountains that the sun couldn't be seen before noon—hardscrabble, coal-mining country, where the air always faintly smelled of coal dust. My mother was in the middle of thirteen children, the only one with jet-black hair, a beautiful woman who benefited from some Cherokee blood three generations back.

My mother clawed her way out of those mountains to become one of the first female accounting professors to teach at Virginia Tech. I can see her so clearly in my head, pounding out the door each morning in alligator high heels, headed for a full day of teaching—all of which she managed on a pack of crackers and a Coke. She seemed to me perhaps what all talented mothers seem to their daughters: larger than life.

The fly in the ointment, though, was that this sharp accountant of a mother had given birth to a word girl. My mother must have wondered if she came home from the hospital with the right baby. I was the spacey pink ballerina who lived inside books, fascinated by the world of ideas and people. I groaned over columns of numbers. If life is an exciting adventure, why would you slow down to count the pegs?

All our lives, we called out across a chasm neither of us

could quite breach, very different women with strong personalities, bound by deep love and, on occasion, fiery conflict. Math mama and word girl, quite the pair.

Accountants deal in a different currency of life—and words are rarely their forte. A craving took ragged shape in me, building momentum all through my thirties. I longed for words. Words of affirmation, or some sort of verbal validation. Those blessing words, I was sure, were the key to unlock all life's good doors, and if I could just get those words from my amazing mother, I could sail out into life with real confidence. Really, I just knew I could—if the words were there.

I might have traded my little finger to hear these words, so deep was the longing: *You can do it. You've got what it takes. Go for it!* Not hearing this encouragement was my own secret wound.

One day, I got down on my knees and asked God if he would please, please bring me words I could hear from another flesh-and-blood person, words I could receive as his very own words to me. Would he please? I didn't know if God actually gave words—but I wanted to get in line if he did.

This is hard to explain, but in a story too long to tell, God answered that strange prayer. Over the course of the next year, in odd moments and completely unbidden, someone would offer me a compliment, a word of affirmation—someone who had no real cause to do that. From out of nowhere, words came, ones I didn't always deserve. But because my ears had been unplugged, I could actually receive them.

Sometimes, those comments would bring little stinging tears to my eyes, because I knew this time, it was God who was opening my ears to hear his word to me, *which can come through so many venues*, once I stopped trying to wring it out of one too-important human being. The great irony is that as my mother aged, she offered more words of affirmation. But I didn't really need them. Once my heart was open, they seemed to come in many other ways.

God would never limit you to one too-important person. That's something to tuck away in your back pocket. God would never limit what you need to one human source. I was a long time learning that.

We all carry a wound like this, often one that comes from real trauma or genuine neglect. Even in the best of life circumstances, it's impossible to make it through a fallen world without being stung to the core of our beings by dark and poisonous darts.

If this is something you sense it would be good to explore, I encourage you to take a blank pad of paper and spend a couple of hours with God—praying and writing. This is a simple process, but it's powerful.

Maybe the wound you carry around is so obvious it's right on the top of your brain. Or maybe not. Just simply ask God what has held you back or gotten in your way or kept you stuck. What has defeated you over and over? And begin to write. Why has that experience been particularly hard? What is there you wouldn't want anyone to know? How has this wound followed you around? What part of it actually deserves a few tears?

What I find amazing about the gospel is that it uniquely acknowledges the depth of the wounding we experience in a fallen world. And the gospel makes the audacious claim that our wounds can be transformed by the love of Christ that flows from his wounds into ours.[62]

The Lie

Our wounds are the breeding ground for lies. And the lies are a much bigger problem than the original wounds. The devil is not called "the father of lies"[63] for nothing. He is wickedly crafty, able to disguise his darkness as light.[64] *As though this lie is the actual, for-real truth about you.* Pain and sin give him camouflage for his deceptions.

The way to find a lie that exerts significant power in your life is fairly simple: *What is the message you believed from the wound in your life?*

For example, what lie did I believe in this verbal vacuum that my amazing mother was unable to fill with the words I thought would make me whole?

You don't have the goods, Paula. The right stuff? You don't have enough of that either. Even worse, honey, you are an impostor, parading about as though you actually have what it takes. And someday, people are going to figure this out. Your inadequacies will start to show, big-time.

And nobody will want to hear a word you have to say.

---

[62] Isaiah 53:5.
[63] John 8:44.
[64] 2 Corinthians 11:14.

I don't have to think hard to write those words. The lies we believe aren't rational little ditties that can be defended in court. But two things are important here:

- **The lies we believe don't have to be true to be powerful.** Think of a conversation you might have had with a friend whose father was an alcoholic. Somehow, you realize she actually believes that if she had been a more lovable little girl, her dad would have sobered up for good.

  You stop her cold. *What? That's crazy.* It's so clear that her father's problem reflected the hellishness of addiction—not her lovableness. That sounds crazy to your ears. And yet, it's the very crazy that has driven her into the arms of a string of undesirable men.

  We can see the irrationality in other people's stories because it's not our own pain. But it's in the moments of personal pain that the devil works his deception. Somewhere in the mayhem, he slips in a lie. We might never fall for such foolishness in the clear light of day. But when we are hurting, we tend to swallow the lie whole.

- **The truly powerful lies in your life are about shame.** It's as though each of us sits at the bottom of a well, staring at a couple of sentences carved into that dark, damp wall. No matter what we know in our heads, these are the actual sentences we live by.

  You really don't have what it takes.

  No one would love you if they knew the truth about you.

Your flaws disqualify you from . . . well, almost everything, really.

This is our "shame story." Each of us has one.[65] Outside the Garden, we come into this fallen world with a sort of existential shame—an original, bone-deep awareness of unworthiness because we've been cut off from God, the source of our very being.

Then life happens. Or rather, it piles on with small betrayals or genuine abuse—something that feels like or is rejection from people we love. The kid at the bottom of the well draws the same conclusion: *Of course, it's me. At the core of my being, these flaws and inadequacies disqualify me from being loved.*

Naming any lie that's had controlling power in our lives can bring us to a place of genuine, kiss-the-ground freedom. Redemption begins with naming bondage. The darkness is brought into the light—and light cleanses. Maybe not all in a single, blazing flash. But the process of stepping into *what can be* in our lives always seems to include naming the lies. The lies we assumed were "truth."

So when you pull out a fresh page and begin writing about which lies have had the biggest grip on you, don't think too hard. You aren't in a laboratory, dissecting your failings. Again, because you have been loved from before the world began, simply ask God, *What lies have I swallowed?*

---

[65] See Brené Brown, "The Courage to Be Vulnerable," interview by Krista Tippett, *On Being*, updated January 29, 2015, https://onbeing.org/programs/brene-brown-the-courage-to-be-vulnerable-jan2015/#transcript.

What lies have been most shaping and influential in your experience?

The more clearly we can name the lies that control, the closer we are to seeing God defeat their power over us. That's why the apostle James said bluntly that we should confess our sins to each other and pray for each other—because down that very path is where we will find healing.[66]

The Choices

If only the lies we believe could be kept in a bottle on a shelf. Or stored in a safe-deposit box. But no: "As [a man] thinks in his heart, so is he."[67] Those little sentences engraved into the wall on the bottom of the well where we live—those beliefs shape our choices. They shape the women we become.

In my case, the lie that some big achievement or some special validation would forever erase my chronic sense of inadequacy created its own little monster. It mutated into a black crow that sat on my shoulder and carped in my ear, *Do more, be more.* An endless quest ensued. If I could just correct my flaws, or perhaps polish things off a bit more (always a bit more), then I'd be okay. Really, I'd be okay.

The "choice" I made out of the lie I believed was to become a cool, aloof, would-be-professor woman who generally sounded like she had a lot of answers. It's as though I stepped back ten feet from everyone who might have eyes to see, and the expert I became was an expert at keeping others at arm's length. My "safe place" was, ironically, anything that

66 James 5:16.
67 Proverbs 23:7, NKJV.

added to the guise of projecting competence. Mostly, it felt like a grand game of pretend.

I wish that I could have kept this malaise just knocking around inside me. But a harsh critical voice like this almost always turns outward, in a critical spirit toward the people closest to us. Certainly, that's been true for me. Word girl can find all sorts of ways to correct your flaws too. It pains me to think of it—how easily the unhealed parts of us come out in words that tear down when we long to build up.

By forty, honestly, I was a quietly angry woman who could barely keep her cynicism contained. And that was scary stuff. No matter how hard I tried, I couldn't get *there* to that "arrived" sort of quiet place where I wasn't so afraid of being exposed as a fake. I couldn't get from the outside world to this blessing thing that would fix my insides.

I knew enough to realize I had to look to God, somehow. But how, really? It seemed like he was holding out on me too. I could not wring a sense of approval from him either. The God of the universe could not be expected to lower his standards to that degree. And so, I stewed in my aloneness, with my veil of competency wearing patchy and thin.

I mention this about God because the truly macabre work of the enemy of our souls is always to distort our image of God. Always. The Bible says that the wages of sin is death[68]—meaning that our sin isn't neutral. It carries us to faraway places where we grow increasingly blind. We project our disappointments with fallen people in a fallen world onto

---

[68] Romans 6:23.

God. *Onto God.* We stumble around believing that this God who gave his Son as our ransom is actually the one who's *withholding* the love we need.

So if you write about where your choices have taken you . . . what comes out the end of your pen? Or if you talk this through with a friend, what do you hear yourself saying? Who do you need to forgive in this process? Are you able to forgive yourself? In what way do some of those choices represent the loss of something that matters to you? Can you ask God to restore and redeem what the locusts have taken away?[69]

Redemption—*what can be*—means God does not leave us with no way out. No—he finds us in our mess and rescues our souls with his truth.

The Truth

Novelist Edith Wharton once said, "What complex blunderers we all are . . . struck blind sometimes, and mad sometimes. . . . Life's just a perpetual piecing together of broken bits."[70] That's a pretty accurate description of life outside the Garden. And what I'm really saying is that no one can piece back together the broken pieces of your soul except the one who made you at the start. And this is a perennial, ongoing process.

In my journey with this, I had a year where I let myself not know the answers. I quizzed other folks about how their hearts got rooted in God's love. And I told God what was

---

[69] Joel 2:25, author's paraphrase. See also verses 26-32.
[70] Edith Wharton, *The Reef* (London: Minerva, 2018), 161.

obvious: that while I could teach a class on all this, I suspected I didn't know the love of Jesus where it counted.

It's like picturing yourself sitting on the curb, holding out an empty tin cup. You are waiting. Hoping. Listening in a new way. This time, I was asking God for the actual truth he was trying to give me. I let myself wonder.

C. S. Lewis said that "God whispers to us in our pleasures" but he "shouts in our pain." God's megaphone rouses us out of our deafness.[71] I found that to be so. A bit of discomfort can remind us to take the cotton out of our ears.

It took a while. Slowly, in the listening, I discovered that the Spirit of God has a scrub brush powerful enough to scrape off the most damning inscriptions in the well of our souls. The blood of Jesus reaches that far. God writes new words of love and acceptance that take shape slowly, always catching us by surprise—a love that seems so impossible, it must be true.

I think in all of Scripture, Isaiah says this in its clearest form. This is what God whispers in our hearts, but truly, he is shouting it from the highest mountain, if only we can hear:

Now thus says the LORD,
he who created you, O Jacob,
   he who formed you, O Israel:
"Fear not, for I have redeemed you;
   I have called you by name, *you are mine*."[72]

---

[71] C. S. Lewis, *The Problem of Pain* (New York: HarperCollins, 2001), 91.
[72] Isaiah 43:1. Emphasis added.

If you belong to someone else, your worth, your significance, your sense of competence no longer depends on you. As I waited with my empty tin cup by the side of the road, I could finally hear that truth: *Maybe, Paula, your life is not about having what it takes—all that "right stuff" business. Maybe, just maybe, belonging to Jesus is so packed with "enough-ness" that it will carry you everywhere you need to go.*

It continues carrying me where I need to go.

Exchanging a lie you believe for the truth God wants you to embrace can sound like a rather solitary experience. And indeed, it does begin between you and God.

But as I found quickly, for truth to get solid inside you, you must risk sharing it with others. Real, flesh-and-blood people who are invited in new ways to know the woman you are—this woman that Jesus knows and still loves. People whose support and encouragement you no longer dismiss but start to count. When you're living in the truth, you learn to let a few more people past the parlor of your life.

One of the concrete things I stumbled on—really, I think God just dropped this on me—was the idea of digging out photos of friends whose voices had been positive and supporting. My own little chorus of cheerleaders—and I think we all have those, if we look. Those women have sat on my bedside table for years now, in ridiculously expensive frames, a collective female reminder that the God of the universe has a thousand ways to wrap me in his goodness and love. And he does the same for you.

This is the sort of redemptive train we board over and over throughout our lives, as God takes us further into *what can be*. The lie we can finally put into words. What we believed about God and ourselves and others—and the dark places those choices take us. But the truth—oh, the truth spells our freedom, though it might make us quite miserable when we first try it on for size.

On this path, the actual story inside us changes. Or, as Curt Thompson said in his wonderful book *The Soul of Shame*, we begin to tell ourselves a different story.[73]

That is almost the definition of deep, redemptive change: *You start telling yourself a different story.*

I wish I could say I lived all my moments in the freedom of belonging to the God who loves me. I wish my tongue never turned sharp and sassy. But this is the evidence of ongoing redemption: I'm able to find home sooner than I used to. I work harder at forgiveness—receiving it myself and offering it to others—because unforgiveness keeps the lie stuck to the walls of my soul. And it's the lie that kills.

Don't miss the power of the gospel let loose in your life. That's the thing to ask God—*What is the truth you want me to receive and carry forward?* That's what you build a life on. Truth taken into the deep places of your heart rearranges the pieces of the way you do life. What you see and experience is redemption—a cool, clear taste of what God has always wanted to bring to life in you.

It's a tragedy to stand knee-deep in water and yet be dying of thirst. Drink fresh water from the river of life that Christ

---

73 Curt Thompson, *The Soul of Shame: Retelling the Stories We Believe about Ourselves* (Downers Grove, IL: InterVarsity, 2015), 112.

claims flows through you by his Spirit.[74] There's so much of God's goodness to be had. Even in the here and now of a broken, bleeding world.

As Moses beautifully wrote in Deuteronomy, this ongoing process of *what can be* is a story that repeats over and over in our lives. May we have eyes to see:

> In the wilderness He fed you manna which your
> fathers did not know, that He might humble you and
> that He might test you, *to do good for you in the end.*
> Otherwise, you may say in your heart, "My power and
> the strength of my hand made me this wealth."[75]

What a thought, really. God longs to bring you through the wilderness and into a place of goodness so rich you would be tempted to think you got there by your own little genius.

Except that you know better.

---

[74] John 7:37-39.
[75] Deuteronomy 8:16-17, NASB. Emphasis added.

Reflections
on

SEEING REDEMPTION IN INTERIOR SPACES

Seeing *redemption* in the here and now means you taste some of God's goodness as you step into new habits and attitudes and choices. Your life opens up to the possibilities of *what can be*. Paula wrote about that internal process in terms of wound, lie, choices, and truth. Let's follow that progression in scriptural form, allowing for some space and time for that to sink into your own story.

WOUND

1. First, listen to the words of David, who was hunted by a jealous King Saul:

   > With my voice I cry out to the Lord;
   >> with my voice I plead for mercy to the Lord.
   >
   > I pour out my complaint before him;
   >> I tell my trouble before him.
   >
   > When my spirit faints within me,
   >> you know my way!

> In the path where I walk
>> they have hidden a trap for me.
> Look to the right and see:
>> there is none who takes notice of me;
> no refuge remains to me;
>> no one cares for my soul.
>
> I cry to you, O LORD;
>> I say, "You are my refuge,
>> my portion in the land of the living."[76]

What wound in your life has caused you to feel isolated, trapped, or unjustly labeled as the "bad" person? What was the impact? What gave that wound such life-shaping power?

LIE

2. If you think about the lie(s) you swallowed in the midst of pain, remember that those lies are usually far from rational. The lies we believe shape how we see God—and how we see ourselves and others.

Before you read the following Scripture passage, take the wound that God has brought to mind and ask him in utter simplicity, "Lord, what lie(s) did I believe as I lived through this wound?" Then start to write and see what comes out the end of your pen.

3. When it comes to believing a lie, we all pantomime the scene of Eve in the Garden, in eerily similar fashion. The enemy of our

---

[76] Psalm 142:1-5.

souls knows our hidden vulnerabilities. Follow this through with Eve and notice what seems too familiar.

> Now the serpent was more crafty than any other beast of the field that the LORD God had made.
> He said to the woman, "Did God actually say, 'You shall not eat of any tree in the garden'?" And the woman said to the serpent, "We may eat of the fruit of the trees in the garden, but God said, 'You shall not eat of the fruit of the tree that is in the midst of the garden, neither shall you touch it, lest you die.'" But the serpent said to the woman, "You will not surely die. For God knows that when you eat of it your eyes will be opened, and you will be like God, knowing good and evil." So when the woman saw that the tree was good for food, and that it was a delight to the eyes, and that the tree was to be desired to make one wise, she took of its fruit and ate, and she also gave some to her husband who was with her, and he ate. Then the eyes of both were opened, and they knew that they were naked. And they sewed fig leaves together and made themselves loincloths.[77]

Name all the ways you can see here in which the devil distorts the truth or casts doubt about the character of God.

4. God's command was that Adam and Eve not eat from one tree in the Garden—the tree of the knowledge of good and evil. In eating of that fruit, Eve came to doubt the goodness of God. *Is God really good? Can I trust him?* What personal, particular forms does that lie take in your own story?

---

77 Genesis 3:1-7.

CHOICES

5.   From the lies we believe, we make choices that often take us to a far country where we experience more wounding and more pain.

When Moses led God's people out of Egypt, the way through the wilderness was not easy. They were often hungry, tired, and thirsty. Everything known and familiar in Egypt was gone. And then, Moses ascended the mountain and disappeared behind a cloud to receive instructions from God. What did the people do?

When the people saw that Moses delayed to come down from the mountain, the people gathered themselves together to Aaron and said to him, "Up, make us gods who shall go before us. As for this Moses, the man who brought us up out of the land of Egypt, we do not know what has become of him." So Aaron said to them, "Take off the rings of gold that are in the ears of your wives, your sons, and your daughters, and bring them to me." So all the people took off the rings of gold that were in their ears and brought them to Aaron. And he received the gold from their hand and fashioned it with a graving tool and made a golden calf. And they said, "These are your gods, O Israel, who brought you up out of the land of Egypt!" When Aaron saw this, he built an altar before it. . . . And they rose up early the next day and offered burnt offerings and brought peace offerings. And the people sat down to eat and drink and rose up to play.[78]

What lie were the people of God believing in Moses' absence? Where did their choices take them?

---

[78] Exodus 32:1-6.

What has that progression from wound to lie to choices looked like in your own life?

TRUTH

6. In that crevice in your heart where you've believed a lie that's brought even more pain, God wants to plant something that feels wonderfully new: *truth*. And it's only God's truth that heals.

I suggest that you take what God has shown you so far and simply sit and ask him what particular truth he wants you to grab hold of. Ask him to unfold that truth over the next few months, even, as you listen in a new way to a God who longs to give himself to you. He is truth. And he will lead you into a more deeply realized awareness that you are loved—really and truly loved.

7. Here are two passages (among many) to carry around with you. How do these words translate into your reality?

> But now thus says the LORD,
> he who created you, O Jacob,
>   he who formed you, O Israel:
> "Fear not, for I have redeemed you;
>   I have called you by name, you are mine."[79]

> See what kind of love the Father has given to us, that we should be called children of God; and so we are. The reason why the world does not know us is that it did not know him.[80]

---

79 Isaiah 43:1.
80 1 John 3:1.

CHAPTER 6

REDEMPTION ALWAYS INCLUDES OTHERS

*You Can't Have Deep Relationships
on the Cheap*

Paula

You can't fully experience the *what can be* aspect of the gospel by yourself. God works in your soul in real ways to heal and cleanse and make new. And the practical reality, then, is that you become much less afraid of other people—and thus more able to love and be loved.

The *way* you experience those fuller relationships, that setting aside of fear, though, is through an increased capacity for vulnerability. It's a bit of a paradox. The word *vulnerable* means "able to be wounded," as we mentioned earlier. But the beauty of the gospel is that over time, God builds a bottom floor into your soul. You belong to the God who made you and who has promised that he will never let you go.[81] Not ever. So you can actually risk more with other people, because if someone fails you—or you fail them—it's not the last word. There's the hope of repair. But even more, a greater love covers you both. You can risk vulnerability—which means you can risk the probability that sooner or later, with someone, you'll feel hurt. And you'll cause hurt.

Vulnerability opens up the possibility of knowing (at least) a few people deeply—and being known by someone else. An older man once said to me, as he reflected on years of following Christ, "I am a wealthy man. My life has been rich with relationships." He realized he'd been able to go deep—to really enjoy people—because the gospel increased his capacity to love and be loved. That's the further goodness of *what can be*—the goodness God offers each of us through redemption.

THE SECRET WEAPON GOD OFFERS

Vulnerability isn't easy, which is why it's often spoken of in terms of courage. When you're vulnerable, you share something of your life with someone—and you never know, really, how that will be received.

We don't want our weakness or sin to be discovered. We don't want to be found out. Shame blocks our path to the soul-liberating relationships we long for. And shame poisons the vulnerability that's necessary in order to even (remotely) love others well.

---

[81] Matthew 28:20.

Into this terribly human mix, God offers a secret weapon. In biblical terms, it's called *humility*. Humility is such a powerful phenomenon that the apostle Peter says we should wrap ourselves in it like it's our favorite everyday dress:

> Clothe yourselves, all of you, with humility toward one another, for "God opposes the proud but gives grace to the humble."[82]

In those places in your life where you fear exposure, as though someone would see you as you are and grimace, God offers a surprisingly durable covering. Humility covers the naked experience of shame and thus makes it possible to flesh out vulnerability. Humility forges a path. Or to change the metaphor a bit, humility flies under the radar of shame.

When my aging mother moved to Raleigh, we both had visions of sweet times together. I'd take her to lunch on some restaurant's sunny patio with the dogwoods in full bloom. Her great-grandchildren would be a comfort. There were so many possibilities. Indeed, we'd had such good times together through our adult lives, there was no reason to think this era wouldn't top it all off.

Except there was this snake in the grass called alcohol. I got my beautiful mother to Raleigh and discovered that what I thought was a little problem with wine was an addiction that controlled her life. An addiction that eventually got her dismissed from her very nice retirement community. (Yes,

---

[82] 1 Peter 5:5. See also Proverbs 3:34.

you haven't lived until you've been "called into the principal's office," not for your teenager but for your parent.)

For the longest time, I drowned in shame. How had I missed this? I'm a therapist, and yet I was in almost as much denial as my mother. It was embarrassing. My friends would say, "Oh, I bet it's wonderful having your mother in town now." And I would look for a table to crawl under because, yes, it should have been wonderful.

Finally, I had to take a deep breath and start saying what was true. (That sentence is almost a textbook definition of vulnerability.) "Well, actually, it hasn't worked out like I thought. My sweet mother has a significant problem with alcohol, and it's about to drive us both around the bend." It's hard to make a picture like this pretty.

Of course, my friends knew that I was aware of the best alcohol-recovery groups in town and just the right addictions counselor. Once again, wrapping my nakedness in humility, I would say, "Yes, we've made the rounds of those resources, but this is very late in the ball game. I am powerless to make this problem go away."

I lack the words to explain this adequately, but embracing vulnerability (by living out humility) saved my sanity. The shame of it all slowly dissolved. It was like watching an iceberg break up into smaller chunks and float out to sea. The hard situation with my mother was what it was. And the love of Jesus was truly enough to hold us afloat—my mother and me—until she was released from this frail body.

Saying what was true, even if it revealed what felt like the ugliness I didn't want anyone to see, did so many good things. It allowed me to stay in the ball game with my mother without a boatload of warm feelings. I came to see that there is real victory in just walking out a difficult season as faithfully as you are able. I was tangibly aware of the mercy of God to cover me in such a time.

This is why God ordains humility as the path to the sort of vulnerability that feels like weakness in the moment but actually becomes true strength. When you allow the simple, humble truth into the light, God pours in grace—a special power that is his alone, but shared with you.

We are all outside the Garden, and we are all afraid of being discovered. So we don't tell the truth about our lives. Our selves. Not very easily, anyway. I think often of the way writer Frederick Buechner put this:

> [We] tell what costs [us] least to tell and what will gain [us] most; and to tell the story of who we really are and of the battle between light and dark, between belief and unbelief, between sin and grace that is waged within us all costs plenty and may not gain us anything, we're afraid, but an uneasy silence and a fishy stare.[83]

If it's true—and it is true—that the love of God wraps us tightly and that he who loves us has pledged to love us to the end, then we can weather the uneasy silence and a whole bunch of fishy stares. God knows. And he will bring

---

[83] Frederick Buechner, *Secrets in the Dark: A Life in Sermons* (New York: HarperSanFrancisco, 2006), 84.

along some flesh-and-blood people, as he did for me, who will look us straight in the eye and say, "Oh my. That must be hard." Just as we will do for another weary soul who needs a word of understanding and whose shame we are no longer so scared to see.

PERMISSION TO NEED

In this journey of vulnerability, one small inner shift is so huge that it's like a tiny movement in the earth's plates on the ocean floor. All the water above moves in response.

This will sound deceptively simple, but trust me, it's not: When a woman takes a deep breath with people who matter to her and begins a sentence with, "I think what I need here is . . . ," something huge shifts inside her.

Those words have been some of the hardest ones I've ever gotten out of my mouth. I have been schooled and coached and conditioned to meet needs—not have them myself. What if my request just hangs out there, glaring and unmet? What if, God forbid, I sound kind of . . . needy?

Most women are fantastically attuned to meeting others' needs. And that's a wonderful thing. Vulnerability, though, opens us up to the other side of that equation. If we are living as daughters of God, for whom Christ died, then God invites us into a life where we can work and serve and give—*and* we can play and rest and receive.[84]

You can't receive, though, if you don't have a need. And

---

[84] I have always loved this phrase that David Seamands thought here, used in his much-loved book, *Healing Grace: Finding Freedom from the Performance Trap* (Indianapolis, IN: Light and Life Communications, 1999).

stepping into something that feels like weakness—that opens the possibility of experiencing hurt—is a recurrent saving theme of the gospel as it's lived out with others.

That's part of what makes Christ's life so compelling. The Son of God could ask his friends to pray for him in the hour of his great need? How amazing. He knew what it was to lay himself bare with others. And he knew the solace of the Father when his friends could not touch the depth of what he was experiencing as he faced the cross.

This God who spoke the world into being came in the frailest human form. The one who leads the stars out at night, as Isaiah wrote,[85] permitted himself to be crucified between two common thieves. He is called the "Lamb of God." What animal is more vulnerable than a lamb? And even in heaven, his wounds are still visible—and he is the "Lamb who conquers." Ultimately, it's the chosen vulnerability of our God that gives us courage.

When I was caring for my mother, I felt like I was failing as a daughter in some ways that were important, at least in this book. The woman before me was one I barely recognized, and I was not the model of patience. I needed the mother I'd known for most of my life to deal with my mother-in-this-state, and here I was, turned into my mother's mother at the moment when I most needed a mother. It was all turned around.

To say to a few close friends (who all had thriving mothers, I might add) that I was "not doing well with this" and "I'm lost

---

85 Isaiah 40:26, author's paraphrase.

and don't know what to do"—well, I would rather have walked on nails barefoot than get those words out of my mouth. Except that I just couldn't face what was before me alone. So even if my friends didn't quite understand (sometimes they don't), I needed to take my place in line as a woman-with-a-need because just to own that helped. It helps because God means for it to help! Just simply letting someone pray for me in this place that felt so like failure made a noticeable difference.

I think this is why Jesus modeled something for us in his worst moments that he knew we would find utterly necessary in our own worst moments. Even if the flesh and blood around you sleep through your request, even if they don't quite understand, you will be more open to God and others if you don't just buck up and soldier on.

You are a finite woman living in a screwed-up world with broken people. How could you not have a need? Having a need is like having a homing device that draws you to God—and to others—and, in that way, opens the doors to *what can be*.

COURAGE TO KEEP NEEDING

Connally

There is intrinsic vulnerability in naming your needs aloud, hoping beyond hope that your listener will help. Still, who wants to risk good old-fashioned, face-flushing humiliation? Some icky form of public shaming? But only humbling yourself like Jesus—oftentimes, buttressed by his strength alone—can open the path to need-naming, shame-mending, and, ultimately, help-receiving. My discovery of this, though, has come through a slightly different angle from Paula's.

My broader education and socialization trained me not to have needs—but not because I was supposed to be busily meeting the needs of the people around me. Sure, there was a genuine nod in that direction, particularly if someone had children. But for women coming of age in a Title-IX era, there has been this other, perhaps unarticulated; expectation that we can and should get our own needs met.

With far greater economic, social, and sexual freedom, we're told to make the most of that freedom. Need more stuff? Make more money. Need more stimulation? Get a more substantial job. Need more meaning? Do something spiritual. Need more pleasure? Pursue more sex. Need more family? Have more kids. Need more corporate power? Lean further in.

Of course, many of us born after the boomers didn't think it was wrong to have needs or to name them. Needs are real. And self-care is a big value. But shame seems to crop up when we have needs that we haven't successfully taken steps to get met. *All these resources and opportunities out there, and you are still needy? Hmmm . . .*

It makes sense, doesn't it? In our modern, Western world, self-sufficient self-actualization holds the (perhaps only) promise of self-satisfaction. So if you can't figure out how to get your own needs met . . . sadly, the implicit conclusion is that there is little hope for you to attain all the yummy things in life, like love, joy, and peace.

Imagine, then, how I felt when I began recognizing that I needed something that good men uniquely bring to the table. My brothers lived overseas; my father was in a different city. Many men at church were married or barely interested in marriage, and most friends' husbands were lovely but understandably not focused on knowing me. And to top it off, I was still single. I knew that I wanted and *needed* that male goodness. But given the dearth of guys built into my life, knowing what to do with that need was a bit tricky.

Even admitting my dilemma was not easy. You see, despite the combination of my mother's loudest protests, some early theological voices, and perhaps even my own natural instincts to the contrary, I had been broadly educated to think of men and women as essentially interchangeable. The only differences between us (beyond the seemingly negligible biological ones) were supposed to be socially constructed and imposed.

Prevailing notions notwithstanding, however, I couldn't help but know that a Saturday night or even a leisurely Sunday afternoon spent in the presence of one or many good men felt palpably different to me from such times without such men. Likewise, getting my brother to pray for me— even if over the phone and long-distance—was somehow different from having my best, even most empathetic and spiritually attuned girlfriend pray with me. (I actually found that getting both parties to pray packed the biggest punch.) And many work meetings seemed to deepen in robustness when women *and* men worked together.

None of this was about men being "better" in some kind of ranking between the sexes. The good women in my life have been and remain more than indispensable. But, I recognized, there is simply a different kind of strength that good men bring with them. Something solidifying, grounding, and, in the best cases, deeply empowering. Still, as time went on, I was facing the reality that, left to its own course, my life could unfold, for all meaningful purposes, basically man-free.

Unfortunately, though, I couldn't just create "good maleness" in my kitchen, on my keyboard, or even in my quiet times with God. *Put me to sleep, take my rib, and please, Jesus, just get me some kind of Adam!*

Enter God's admonition for humble trust. Exposing my presupposition that men bring a unique kind of strength that I not just wanted but needed—and couldn't get on my own—felt risky. I might be setting myself up for not just a few eye-rolling scoffs but possibly for accusations of some vague cultural transgression. Perhaps I would earn my own scarlet letter, a *B* for Backwoods or Binary or Both. And why would a people pleaser like me risk going public with perceived foolishness, let alone potential socio-moral failure, particularly if there were no guarantees of that need getting met?

I'd risk these things because without asking, there was no other way to receive. There were just no other paths available. So repeatedly swallowing that initially bitter mixed drink of pride and fear, I began practicing saying aloud the thing that felt, for a host of reasons, unallowable.

"Hi, my name is Connally, and I need good male strength in my life, in lots of forms. And I can't make it happen on my own. Will you help me?"

In theory, such a statement promises to do the trick, sneaking by shame and opening the door to something more. At least until one actually utters the words. Inevitably, even the most relationally aware and kind man in the mix can't help but respond with something incredibly, dare I say, *male*.

"Help me," asked my supervisor, "to know what that means. What would this look like for you?"

Awkward. What was I thinking in voicing this? I remember reaching for answers to his reasonable question, painfully realizing that I was far more of an English major than an engineer:

"Well, Don, it's like a good man can be a bass drum or a plumb line. You know? He can be like an anchor on one hand or a bow of the boat on the other. And I need these things in my life, even as a capable single woman. Does that make sense?"

Bless that man. He stayed in the conversation long enough for me to find a few more mutually accessible words for what I was trying to say. He helped me translate my metaphors into concrete to-dos for him. In this case, that meant checking in with me more regularly, asking about the areas in my life where I felt weak (this was particularly important for me at that juncture), praying for me, and doing his special magic of helping me pull together my thoughts.

It's not that a woman couldn't do any of these things—many girlfriends and I have done and continue to do just these sorts of things for one another. But there was something about *him* doing this, as a *man*, in his intrinsic *maleness*, that was its own unique contribution. I fear I still can't explain it very well. One's sexuality is such a sensitive subject in our culture right now. And perhaps even more to the point, the mystery of God imaging himself in both male and female is hard to nail down in words. Still, the intrinsic contribution of not just his personhood but his him-ness was undeniable.

All this to say, in an epoch of gender confusion and dissolving extended families, it's an unnerving time to be a woman who realizes that she needs good men in her life *and* that her "asking" for that goodness is part and parcel to her receiving. It can feel so vulnerable. Yet as I have continued asking (a little more subtly and effectively over time), I have begun to see God's provision in ways that I simply couldn't have predicted.

Growing up, I had no categories (let alone models) for single women who had men meaningfully woven into their lives. But God has brought a brother here, a brother there. Not just my original family brothers (though I'm grateful for the good they bring), but people like a dear man with whom I serve on a board at a graduate theological college. He is like a brother to me; I consult with him on a regular basis for brotherly input, even as I offer him my input, oftentimes on leadership decisions, in return.

I think, too, of a few professors at that same theological college. When I'm with them, the presence of these good men often strengthens me. (It helps, I believe, that their wives are my friends.) Or I think of the couple with whom I lived for more than ten years. During one season of great anxiety in my life, the husband, George, would sit and watch TV while I worked puzzles. His presence was medicinal. The list could go on—a financial adviser whose path I crossed in the last few years. "I have a heart for middle-aged single women navigating their finances," he told me. Okay, I gulped at that moniker. But honestly, I've needed exactly what he has had to bring. Oh, and then there has been the sweet, fatherly lawyer whose surprising pro bono gift to me was to help me navigate my housing contract gone deeply south. You get the idea.

Of course, none of these men treat me like a special lover. I'm not anyone's wife. There is potential expression of good, male intimacy that is not open to me. Some longings remain unmet (true for every human being on the planet, so I'm not alone in this). Still, I need the strength that the presence of good men can bring. And the amazing thing is, as I've been willing to ask, God has kept providing it. There really *can be* a surprising gift of manna, nourishing me, helping me go forward, step by step, yet undaunted, even in the relational and gender wilderness of our culture.

BONDS OF GRATITUDE

Humility can powerfully plow a path to need-naming, shame-mending, and help-receiving, but it has one more trick up its sleeve, as well. Humility can help build the bonds of gratitude.

My mother was the first one to teach me to write thank-you notes—to grandparents or aunts and uncles, mostly for Christmas gifts. From early on, I just knew I was supposed to do this. Like replacing the toilet paper roll, writing thank-you notes was simply what a person did to be considerate of others.

When I was about twenty-five, however, I learned from a friend in Philadelphia one of the deeper *whys* behind such considerate expressions of thanks. This friend, Pete, had worked for nonprofits for a while, and by his own admission, he hated writing thank-you notes. His handwriting was chicken scratch. He could never find stamps when he needed them. Plus, part of him reasoned, people knew he was grateful. His organization was good about sending out generalized thank-yous on his behalf. But he went on to explain, he still did it.

Pete wrote thank-you notes because in so doing, something magical transpired. He grew more aware with each note that he neither owned nor was owed the world or its resources, *but* that somebody out there had actually *chosen* to offer a bit of the world's resources to him. Something in his posture changed with each note he wrote. The very act of humbly expressing gratitude seemed to grow his humility and gratitude. And this, in turn, seemed to open Pete to seeing the givers less as "giving units" and more as people. His humility opened his eyes wide in appreciation for his human helpers *and* the God whose hands they were in.

Pete's was a primarily professional context. But in personal contexts, it is the same. "Thank you" can tighten the ties between us.

When it came time for my mother to move from her very large home of forty years, I nearly collapsed with panic. For various reasons, my brothers could not be there except for about ten days during the six months preceding the move. And I knew the work that needed to be done to get the house on the market, not to mention the sheer volume of things to be gingerly sorted (my mom was an art-history major, so most objects in her possession were deeply imbued with emotion, history, and meaning), was absolutely beyond our capacity to handle on our own.

To the degree either my mother or I had had trouble up to that point naming needs or asking for help, frankly, we just had to get over it. Pride and fear couldn't just be swallowed; they had to be tossed out the window. Gargantuan needs can be clarifying.

One month after her move, I counted sixty-six people who had shown up to help us in the previous four months. Sixty-six. Most testified to my parents' long-term commitment to their church and community. You couldn't have counted all the footsteps that crossed our threshold bearing and carrying dinners and duct tape, boxes and brooms. Teenagers waxed floors; neighbors loaned tools; girlfriends sorted linens or books; family members cleaned out cobwebs; and men with trucks hauled wrought-iron furniture, bookcases, and an endless array of unwieldy objects to new homes. One friend even showed up every day, tools in tow. He'd done disaster relief professionally. Need I say more about my gratitude?

When I finally sat down to write a massive thank-you

note (honestly, I did not have the bandwidth to compose sixty-six individual ones), I was dumbfounded. Typing my words about gratitude, I realized that this outpouring of service had bonded me to these sixty-six people in a way that I could never have anticipated. The sixty-six hadn't become my insta-BFFs, of course. But scrolling through that email list, I recognized a deepened softness in my heart as my eyes rolled over each name. Having just moved back to my hometown after twenty-eight years away, I exhaled. I'd been granted a reweaving into this loose-but-committed community that I hadn't even known I needed. I was awestruck.

HELP, THANKS, WOW

Author Anne Lamott has a book entitled *Help, Thanks, Wow: The Three Essential Prayers*. This woman has nailed it with her title.

Help, Thanks, Wow. These are the relational movements that characterize redemption lived out in our relationships. In a sense, the "Wow" in relationships is simply the deep sigh of amazement. It's the response to the beauty we've seen when we've risked humbling ourselves, broken out past shame's jail keeper, asked for help, and received something good. "Wow" is what Paula said when she risked telling the truth about her mom and found herself helped. "Wow" was my response when I risked asking on one hand for good male strength and on the other for help in the exhausting work of moving and, in ways I could not have predicted, found myself helped.

Really, *Wow* is another word for the worship that flows from our lips and through our lives into the world around us. It is our acknowledgment—often in joy, but even in the crucible of help (and hope) deferred—of the bigness and goodness of God. "Wow" is our response to the God in whose redemption we can walk, with others, even on this messy planet. It's the gift given back to the one who lets us taste something of what life with and in Jesus Christ can be now.

Reflections
on

REDEMPTION ALWAYS INCLUDES OTHERS

1. Living into the redemptive *what can be* of your life always includes others. This counters the modern myth that if you really have your act together, you (or, at most, you and God) are all you really need. In what ways do you find yourself taken in by the idea that you are—or ought to be—enough? What does it cost you?

2. There are almost sixty versions of "one another" verses in the New Testament. Here are three that appear most commonly:[86]

    I, therefore, a prisoner for the Lord, urge you to walk in a manner worthy of the calling to which you have been called, with all humility and gentleness, with patience, *bearing with one another in love* . . .[87]

    Let the word of Christ dwell in you richly, *teaching and admonishing one another* in all wisdom, singing psalms

---

[86] Andrew Mason, "The 59 One Anothers of the Bible," Small Group Churches, accessed June 1, 2019, http://www.smallgroupchurches.com/the-59-one-anothers-of-the-bible/.
[87] Ephesians 4:1-2. Emphasis added.

and hymns and spiritual songs, with thankfulness in your hearts to God.[88]

But *encourage one another every day*, as long as it is called "today," that none of you may be hardened by the deceitfulness of sin.[89]

3. Scripture simply does not recognize a life in the body of Christ that is not lived out in relational community. How has your life been shaped—or have you helped to shape the life of someone else—in some "one another" way, even in the past week?

4. Paula and Connally wrote about having permission to need something from others. It's really the courage to receive, as well as to give. What makes receiving a challenge for you at some points? What happens in you when you take a deep breath and voice a need, knowing that it may not be met like you hoped? How does a step of vulnerability and growth actually open up redemptive possibilities and strengthen your faith in God?

5. Humility is like a secret weapon that flies us under the radar of shame. It's the antidote to that very human desire to hide our inadequacy and our sin. When you have owned a need or shared some way in which you've failed with another person, and perhaps even asked for prayer, what have you experienced? What changed in you in that process?

6. In one of the worst moments of Christ's life, he longed for the support of his friends. Three times, he asked his closest friends to stay awake and pray for him, while he wrestled with the

---

88 Colossians 3:16. Emphasis added.
89 Hebrews 3:13, MOUNCE. Emphasis added.

Father, facing the cross. Three times, he returned from praying to find that his friends had fallen asleep (Matthew 26:36-46). What does this story say to you about your own human need for others, and what encouragement do you draw from Christ's experience here?

7. Gratitude toward God spills over into gratitude with others, and relationships flourish. Consider these two passages. What would it mean for gratitude to mark your life in a deeper way?

> Let them thank the Lord for his steadfast love,
>   for his wondrous works to the children of man!
> And let them offer sacrifices of thanksgiving,
>   and tell of his deeds in songs of joy.[90]

> Through him then let us continually offer up a sacrifice of praise to God, that is, the fruit of lips that acknowledge his name. Do not neglect to do good and to share what you have, for such sacrifices are pleasing to God.[91]

---

90 Psalm 107:21-22.
91 Hebrews 13:15-16.

CHAPTER 7

SAYING YES TO GOD

Where Might That Yes Take You?

Connally

Something about the "Wow" of our worship for God doesn't just bubble up inside us for ourselves alone. There is more to the redemption that Jesus brings than the delicious soul-drenching of supernatural champagne. Rather, the "Wow" of worship is created to spill redemptively into the world around us.

So spill it does. By its very nature, it has to. The Spirit of God pours into us like a river of life once we've entered into the redemption that Jesus brings. And none of us can contain that river. *What can be* flows through us into the world.

Sometimes the spillage sparkles before your eyes, the glistening overflow of your long-held dreams. Since you were young, beauty has always caught your attention. Amazingly, three years out of school, you find yourself starting a small interior-design firm. Alternatively, you're drawn to a more contemplative life, and you find yourself interceding for those whose lives are miles or even generations away from yours. Your prayers pour out like underground rivers, and one day they spring up in another life, in another place.

Or maybe as a child, you were inexorably drawn to the stories you read. Your imagination was captivated, formed even, by tales of noble good battling insidious evil. And now, wonder of wonders, you find yourself working in a film studio, teaching high-school English, or making up tales to tell your nieces and nephews on a warm summer night. Perhaps even that passel of children who are forever under your feet are the embodiment of your dreams spilled out into the world.

Conversely, sometimes the redemption that flows through you has little to do with any dreams. It's akin, instead, to that which gushes into and eventually through your life when some dam breaks, when you find yourself washed up on some foreign shore you never hoped for. Your big loss—of job or friend, husband or health—floods your heart with grief. But somehow, your hard-earned familiarity with salty tears ends up pouring out as the gift of empathy to those around you.

Or maybe, as your life or even community is swamped with challenges matching the stuff of your nightmares, new strengths emerge. Suddenly, you're writing editorials for a cause that was never on your radar before. You're teaching a class for a group of people who a decade earlier would have never gotten your attention. You're in a laboratory, researching the cure to a disease whose ravages you long to stop.

More often than not, God's goodness flows into and through our lives in multiple ways, embodying our dreams and, by his grace, using our hardest journeys. As a result, it spills out in an endlessly shifting kaleidoscope of expressions. Always, *what can be* is designed to look something like bringing God's goodness to the people and places around us.

WHEN DREAMS AND BROKEN DAMS WORK TOGETHER

Earlier, I told the story of the goodness of confronting *what is* with my housemate, Maria—the dam-breaking tensions that surfaced between us, uprooting deep weeds in my heart. When Maria and I moved to different living situations, we remained friends. Yes, she remained black and I white. We had never feigned color blindness. Still, together, we had leaped forward in the journey of seeing each other with the eyes of our shared Redeemer.

Fourteen years later, suffering the rapid ravages of pancreatic cancer, Maria joked with me about beating me in the race, getting to see the eyes of our shared Redeemer in person first. With tenderness, we laughed about still being competitive after all those years. A few days before she died, she wrapped her thin arms around my neck, and our teary words with each other were as real and heartfelt as those of sisters. Maria and I looked each other in the eye and blessed each other. Forever.

My friendship with Maria has continued to shape me in

the ensuing years. Perhaps the biggest gift she gave me—through our wrestling, love, and breakthrough—has been the realization that the very places of our sin and brokenness can, with God's grace, transform into paths of life. Not only for ourselves but also for others.

What is really can morph into *what can be*.

Forced out of denial, I have been increasingly set free to talk candidly, personally and publicly, about essential identity and racial issues. My fear of being outed for my secret sin has almost melted away. And I've been given continued opportunities for contribution, often out of the blue.

My old friend Sherry has reemerged from our time working together years ago at the Center for Urban Theological Studies. She and I have found ourselves speaking on these topics of race at events and conferences. Likewise, I've had the opportunity to do graduate work on the topic of the divisions in the black and white American church. Meanwhile, right when I was thinking about changing jobs, a national role addressing faith and diversity questions within my organization emerged. Even now, I get to help others navigate racial tensions in ministry settings, as well as in personal friendships. I can imagine Maria laughing and saying, "That's right! You owe me, girl. It wasn't easy being your friend, but you've come a long way!"

I'm making a complex story simple. The pathway is rarely simple in practice. But you get the idea. *What is* never has to be the end of the story. When Jesus enters the mess, ashes can be exchanged for beauty. And against what seems to be all odds, that beauty can be a gift to others.

WORK AS AN OFFERING

At the start of this book, Paula and I discussed how life *ought* to be. Genesis revealed a Garden in which there was its own commission, God's bidding to rich worship, real human bonds, and meaningful work.[92] What we've been trying to show in these last few chapters is that the redemption of Jesus Christ, into which we get to start living now, offers us tastes of the Garden, so to speak. We get to partake in rich worship—offering God the "Wow" of our gratitude. We get to build real human bonds, particularly as we find his strength to be vulnerable with others. And we can discover meaningful work as we commit to keep moving, even through the mess, to bring tastes of the Garden to others.

For a long time, many Christians emphasized solely the goodness of worship and human bonds, setting aside the idea of work or God's calling (beyond, say, to the mission field). Some people had gotten confused and thought work itself was a product of the curse, not just its victim, and therefore not worth the focus. But then, one day, people woke up and said, "But, um, what about that stuff we are doing eight to ten hours a day at the office?" And a few homemakers joined in—"Yes, how about when the big family gathering on a Sunday afternoon is over, and we're folding yet another load of laundry? Does our work matter?" The answer is yes—the work we get to do is (despite

---

92 See N. T. Wright, *The Challenge of Jesus: Rediscovering Who Jesus Was and Is* (Downers Grove, IL: InterVarsity Press, 1999), 183.

the darn recurring weeds and thistles) meant to be a gift to us *and* the means of fleshing out love for our neighbor. Our work does matter to God.

Propelled by an ever-deepening sense of "Wow," we want our energies to spill out into life for others. Every mom I've known who has mashed up organic peas to create healthy baby food for her infant hopes it will contribute to that child's lifetime health. Likewise, the women I've known who are working on Capitol Hill in DC really want to see their policy efforts bring goodness (like education equity or justice or life) to those they affect. And there is not a missionary out there who, longing for none to be shut out from the presence of God, doesn't hope that her words about Jesus will open the door of redemption to those with whom she speaks.

We all know, though, that it doesn't always happen this way. Not all our labors will be a joy or bear the fruit we hope. The fall of our first parents gave the snake a place in the grass, and though ultimately beaten, he does still thrash about. Kids get sick, policies end up shredded on the congressional floor, and missionaries get kicked out of countries.

Here, though, is the doubly amazing thing. Not only can our labors love our neighbors—near and far—but when our labors go bust, the redemption of Jesus doesn't stop. Think about the apostle Paul. While it's not apparent whether he made it to Spain on a missionary journey, he clearly dreamed of going that far west with the Good News of Jesus. That longing appeared to burn in his bones. Likewise, I can only imagine that the prospect of going to prison or living under house arrest might have qualified as some form of nightmare for Paul.

But think for a moment of the impact of Paul's life in the form of letters written during his times of captivity (not to mention the ministry he had among those whose paths he crossed during those times).[93] He longed to be on the road, but his words scratched out in the interim are so charged with God's beauty and authority, they've continued to multiply for centuries upon centuries. In other words, the Lord is kind *and* powerful enough to bring his goodness, his beauty, through even the ashes of our best-laid plans.

In the end, we can return to hope again and again. The redemption that flows through our lives and into the spaces and places and people around us is not, ultimately, all up to us. God's Spirit pours in and through us, but his purposes continue even when our efforts are thwarted. His goodness is a strong and broad river. It takes twists and turns, but it will not be stopped. Our responsibility, though not an easy one, is simply to be willing to swim with his current.

SAYING AN ACTUAL YES

Paula

This is one of the more amazing aspects of seeing God's *what can be* redemption in our lives: that as we drink of the living water pouring into us in Jesus, some of that same living water begins to flow *through us* . . . into others.

---

93 See Ephesians, Philippians, Colossians, and Philemon.

When I first became a Christian, this goodness sharing was actually one of my great fears. Like, oh my stars, maybe what flowed through my soul would morph me into an obnoxious person pushing Jesus on unsuspecting people. Maybe I would drown people in misbegotten enthusiasm.

Okay, maybe I did drown a few. But in general, sharing redemption works out a bit differently. The living water of God that pours through you seeks a more natural outlet. Some of your old loves get transformed into new, Jesus-shaped ventures. And some of your worst nightmares, your deep griefs, burst forth with a passion that shocks the living daylight out of you.

This overflow is rarely the result of setting out to do a great thing for God. He doesn't need you all that much, truthfully. God, the Father, has promised to make his Son, Jesus, known to the absolute ends of the earth. In the last chapter of his story, every knee is already bowed in the praise of his Son. You and I—well, we are along for the ride. It's not that we have to lend a hand to keep the cause afloat, but rather, we get to have a tiny piece of what God is already doing. We are, as the wonderful old hymn[94] claims, standing on the promises of God.

The odd part is that whatever your tiny piece is, it begins in a hidden chamber inside your own heart where, however feebly, you are saying yes to God. *Yes.*

That little voice of yes in me took the shape of writing, early on, when I was especially aware that I had no

---

[94] Russell Kelso Carter, "Standing on the Promises of Christ My King," 1886, public domain.

background or training for this, really. It felt like stepping off the edge of a cliff, or following the scent of a first love. I had been mentored through the pages of books as surely as if someone sat down with me over a hundred cups of coffee. Books were like food. My college friends would head for the beach over spring break, and I would take my stack of C. S. Lewis and his assorted author friends and sit on my back porch and read hours on end, in bliss.

I told my eight-year-old granddaughter that story recently. She's another book lover, so she thought about it a long minute. And then she said, "I think I'll go to the beach when I'm in college—and take my stack of books with me." She would improve on my model. I hadn't the heart to tell her that not much book reading happens on your average college spring break.

Anyhow, it's a rather natural outlet to see God take your original love of something, one of those perhaps forgotten dreams, in a new direction. I was drawn to writing like I was being pulled on a string.

There have been times, though, when honestly, the process has nearly undone me. Sitting down in a tiny room in my garage to confront the blank page on a screen, every doggone day—you have to be crazy to do this. That's what I'd tell myself. I soon learned why so many of the "real writers" are fledgling alcoholics. They wrote in the morning . . . and drank in the afternoon as they edited what they'd written. I understood how that could happen. Writing can fillet you wide open. Old memories surface. Every place you've failed another living, breathing soul—it's all staring you in the face.

And then there are the days when not a word you've written is salvageable. Or the times when there's so much swirling in your head you can't begin to get it down and you sit before the blank screen for days on end. You're convinced the problem is that you are just too plain dumb. On those days, I am prone to kill the small black bugs known to inhabit my office, and I line their carcasses on the windowsill for comfort. I did get something done that day. I did.

But still, you keep saying yes to God and to yourself, and one thing leads to another. Uzziah, one of the better kings of Judah, has been my go-to guy through the years when writing just seems impossible. He became a king of Judah at the age of sixteen, a know-nothin' guy from the hills with no expertise of which to speak. His story in 2 Chronicles lays out the skills he acquired. He built towers in the wilderness, amassed a sizable army, and developed a fertile valley as only a man who loved the soil could.

One phrase from Uzziah's life, though, has reverberated in my head. I think it's the secret that explains the man: "He was marvelously helped, till he was strong."[95] I cannot count the times I've prayed that phrase while twisted into a pretzel, trying to write. *Oh, God, that I would be marvelously helped in this thing that I am not strong enough to do well.*

Then I stop for a minute and remember the verse that follows, as my own warning: "But when he was strong, he grew

---

[95] 2 Chronicles 26:15.

proud, to his destruction."[96] Maybe that's why, in thirty years of writing, I have only once, in the last month, referred to myself as a write-r. I don't think of myself as the noun—just the verb. I write. I write because it's my yes to God and he seems to make it happen (eventually). But a writer? I tread lightly on wrapping any part of myself around that distinction. I don't want to hang my identity there. I hope, until the end of my days, to simply be this woman who is marvelously helped into something that feels like strength. *Lord, if you would just give me words that honor you. That is all I'm asking.*

I find this is a recurrent theme in the lives of people whose worship overflows into a contribution that blesses others. They have a chronic awareness that there is just not enough talent in their bones equal to the task before them. Whether it's arranging flowers or teaching children, the vision they see is beyond their ability to perform.

That pressed-to-the-wall feeling becomes the reminder that God has your back. He will take your five loaves and two fishes and make them into enough to feed a crowd. You don't ever quite see how he makes it happen. But for those who keep saying yes, sometimes the thing just takes off like it has the wind of God beneath it. In writing, I know those moments as ones where I reread a page and I realize, quite clearly, that this is better than I can write. You have known times like that too. You were marvelously helped, and all you can do is say, "Thank you."

On some stray occasion you least expect, someone writes

---

96 2 Chronicles 26:16.

you a note or walks up to you at a conference. The effort you gave—or the words you wrote—pulled this person out of a black hole or gave her the courage to go forward. The living water God poured into you overflowed. It brought God-created life into being.

You get a glimpse of where saying yes can go, what it can be. But only a glimpse—always, only a glimpse.

A WOMAN WHO SAYS YES

One woman in Scripture is so known for saying yes to God that she comes to mind immediately: Mary, the mother of Jesus. I always have to remind myself that Mary was just a girl when the angel appeared to her. What must it have been like to be startled by such a light and hear a voice speaking words like they had been planned from Creation? This angel called her by name. *Mary.* He said that she would conceive a child, unmarried though she was, and that this child, Jesus, would be the Son of the Most High, after David's line, and his Kingdom would never end. The whole panoply of history would find its flesh-and-blood home first in her womb.

I think I would have asked a bunch of questions. Mary was not so inclined. Into this great unknowing, Mary spoke her first yes, the one for which she is most known: "I am the servant of the Lord; let it be to me according to your word."[97]

For Mary, that was only the beginning of saying yes, of course. Her belly began to swell with child. People started

---

[97] Luke 1:38.

to talk. Joseph stood by her, good man that he was, though it took an angel to convince him God was in this. God was, quite literally, in this. But for Mary, young and pregnant and unmarried, carrying this special child must have meant, also, the chronic loneliness of being misunderstood.

Really, Mary's story only gets wilder from there. How, exactly, could she make sense of the Most High allowing his Son to be born in a barn? And then there was that old man's prophecy that, indeed, God's salvation would come through this child, but that a sword would pierce her heart in the process. Oh, to live your whole adult life knowing that both glory and pain await you, dark clouds on a bright horizon, and never know when they will overtake? Over and over, Mary said yes to God and walked forward.

Maybe this yes, said in the face of so much mystery and unknown, was the centerpiece of Mary's call—of her vocation.

Do you remember that strange moment when she was caught in a crowd of people who were clamoring to hear her son? She couldn't get near her own son. So she sent word, and in the ancient Middle East, the extended family was the most important social unit. One mother's voice would have mattered.[98] But what did she get back, through a messenger, no less?

Jesus replied, "Who is my mother, and who are my brothers?" He then opened his hand toward his disciples and said, "Here are my mother and my brothers! . . . Whoever does

---

98 Zondervan Academic, "What Was Family Life Like in New Testament Times?," January 25, 2018, https://www.biblegateway.com/blog/2018/01/what-was-family-life-like-in-new-testament-times/.

the will of my Father in heaven is my brother and sister and mother."[99]

In that moment, Jesus was making it clear—to the one whose very blood gave life to his, no less—that something was unfolding that would trump even family blood. I wonder what Mary did with Jesus' response. Did his words, which foreshadowed a new kind of family forged in his own blood, cut Mary? The son she loved was making it clear that his life was not centered on her. Though his mother, she would now be asked to follow him.

And follow him she did, to the very end of the road, to a cross on a lonely hill. To be the mother of the man on the cross *is* to carry your own cross. To bear the piercing of the one she bore *is* to be pierced. This was Mary's hardest yes of all. She became the mother of a son in great suffering—suffering she could only witness, not remove.

This thing of saying yes to God's call leads to a fuller experience of *what can be*. It leads to places replete with glory and wonder—as it did for Mary. It gives birth to a life of meaning and influence that we would scarcely have imagined. The road there is a narrow one, to be sure, but we are not alone on the path. Not at all. We go in the company of Jesus and the innumerable hosts who have themselves risked saying yes again and again, trusting that the fruit we bear is ultimately up to him.

---

[99] Matthew 12:48-50.

Reflections

on

SAYING YES TO GOD

1. What about the goodness of God—seen in your life or someone else's—has brought a "Wow" of worship to your lips? Tell more about this. What else prompts you to worship God? What does worship look like in your life?

2. More often than not, God's goodness flows into and through our lives in multiple ways, embodying our dreams and, by his grace, using our hardest journeys. How have either your dreams or your struggles been used by God for good in your life or the lives of others? What has this taught you?

3. "We are," Paul says to the Ephesians, "God's workmanship, created in Christ Jesus for good works, which God prepared beforehand, that we should walk in them."[100] What gifts and talents has God given you that you might love your neighbors? What has using these talents been like so far? Looking forward, what contribution to God's purposes in the world (or the life of the person next door) do you sense God might have next for you?

---

[100] Ephesians 2:10.

4. Sometimes, of course, our labors go bust. How have you seen the redemption of Jesus cascade into the lives of others *in spite* (or even because) of your flaws or failures? What does this teach you about the redemptive power of Jesus Christ?

5. Mary, Jesus' mother, said yes to God. As you have time, read the referenced passages and consider what it might have been like to be in Mary's shoes. As a young teen mother?[101] As the mother of a son moving out in a divine calling?[102] As the mother of a son crucified on the cross?[103] What experience with saying yes to God have you had? In what specific way(s) is he asking you to follow him today? Are you willing to say yes and move forward?

6. We go forward in the company of Jesus and the innumerable hosts who have themselves risked saying yes again and again. What effect does it have on you to realize that you are always journeying *with* Jesus Christ, the host of cheering saints who have gone before you, and—much of the time—others who also risk saying yes? What might it mean to recognize that the actual fruit of your obedience is up to the Lord? Take some time to thank him for journeying with you and carrying the ultimate responsibility for fruitbearing in your life.

---

[101] Luke 1:26-52.
[102] John 2:1-12 and Matthew 12:46-50.
[103] John 19:16-30.

What Will Be

RESTORATION

WE'VE BEEN TREKKING TOGETHER through the broad landscape of the Good News of Jesus. Can you stop for a moment to consider how far we've come? As we've been unpacking the first three "chapters" of the four-chapter gospel—Creation, Fall, Redemption, and Restoration—are you beginning to sense how big this dance really is?

We know we were created for something more than much of what we experience, and we rightly long for life as we sense that it was meant to be—warm and rich family meals with no kicks under the table, so to speak. Simultaneously, most of us bang against hard and unyielding places in our lives where our best prayers and most loving labors seem fruitless. It is what it is, no matter what we do.

Still, even when we're about to give way to a sort of dreamless, cut-my-losses mind-set, moments of breakthrough happen. Mind-boggling joy can erupt. Life can be different. Miraculous shifts really do happen.

As we journey forward from this place, then, questions can begin to sound within us: *So what internal posture do I take as I go forward?* Should we primarily long for more, brace for what is, or bank on miracles?

In some sense, the answer to all of it is simply yes. Going forward in the journey, we forever find ourselves dancing between longing, bracing, and banking.

But at the same time, there is one more chapter, without which this whole, big gospel story is incomplete. There is one more mountain peak whose presence affects everything.

This is the promised restoration of all things. The fourth chapter of the gospel is the promise of *what will be*: a new heavens and a new earth.[104] This is the time in the journey when all will be set right.

The redemption that has begun will one day consummate when Jesus Christ returns to judge evil once and for all. He's going to finally and fully establish a new heavens and new earth. Reigning with unbounded love and authority, he will make things whole for those who are in him—in ways far beyond our wildest imaginings. This is the guarantee of our good Father. So as we journey between the *now* and the *still to come*, we are beckoned to discover the strength and joy of this rock-solid hope.

From wherever we sit today, when our eyes gaze on this mountain peak at the end of the journey, something more than longing, bracing, or banking can happen. Something like a sustainable hope in the goodness of God can begin to bubble up in the very here and now. Our pains or joys find themselves rightsized. Something about this final mountain peak radiates the knowledge that today's life is not the endgame, and this can begin to sound within us as Very Good News.

And so the question as we journey becomes: *What would it look like for the hope of tomorrow to play out in life's nooks and crannies, even today?*

---

[104] Isaiah 65:17; 2 Peter 3:13.

CHAPTER 8

HOW HOPE PLAYS BACKWARD

*Little Tastes of Goodness Leave You
Hungry for More*

Connally

I am sitting on a little wooden folding chair at an outdoor wedding. It's seventy-eight degrees. Beautiful, lilting breezes. Pale-blue sky. Dimming horizon. Bugless. Really, this day is all that you might hope for in a central-Virginia outdoor wedding at the end of May. Gorgeous people, gorgeous setting. And with the exception of a gaggle of twentysomething single women sitting on the other side of the aisle, everyone around me seems to be paired with a significant other or laughing with their children.

As I listen to the minister preach about the unique joys of marriage, I watch heads toss back in laughter and nod with knowing smiles, and it starts to gnaw in me. *How have I for fifty years (or at least twenty-five) managed to miss being part of the story that everyone seated in these folding chairs is celebrating? Glorious youth, leaving and cleaving!*

Amid all that sumptuous beauty, a familiar ache creeps in. *Connally, you are not in the story. You don't have a place in the story that people have celebrated in culture after culture, context after context, for time immemorial.*

This thought does not feel good.

But fifteen years of the practice of looking for Jesus amid such feelings reminds me that this is a moment to ask for help. So I resist the pull into some emotional black hole. I silently cry out a rather simple, *Help.*

What emerges would not classify as "vision" in any medieval-mystic sense. Still, I look up, past the minister, to a barn set in the distant, lush green hills, and I can see in my heart's imagination the presence of Jesus—big as that statue of him in Rio de Janeiro. It is as if he is saying, *Connally, you are in the story. You are in the very, very big story of which this moment, this wedding, this couple is simply an icon, an image. This story is vast, eternal, and real—as is my love for you. Gaze on that couple up front and know that like that groom is loving his bride, I am loving my people.*

There are no mighty peals of thunder, no voices of a great multitude. Actually, the only sounds I hear are those of the duet singers. But for one moment, I really inhabit the words in the book of Revelation—that history is headed somewhere, to the marriage supper of Jesus and his bride, his people. To a time when all things are made new.[105] And for one moment,

---

[105] Revelation 19:6-9.

as human wedding singers sing, I am there—seen, known, cherished . . . the beloved bride. It's not an abstract concept. It's reality, and somehow, the eyes of my heart can see.

Something in me exhales. My heart rate slows. My chin lifts slightly. My brow unfurrows. Quietly, I sigh and look around me. The early-evening sky is still pale blue. Breezes still lilt around me. Men still have their arms around wives and girlfriends. The pastor is still speaking about marriage and its glories. And in the distance, the barn is still a barn, with no actual twenty-five-foot statue of Jesus standing above it.

But for one brief moment, I have been reminded—and in turn rehearted, if there is such a word. *God exists. He loves me. And I, along with so many others—from all tribes and peoples—am in the big Story that really is headed somewhere.*

Something really did shift in me that day. It was more than a moment of reminding; those words from Jesus really brought a heart shift. As the wedding spilled into drinks in the magnolia garden and a dinner under a tent, I found myself *wanting* to celebrate the marriages that were around me. Frankly, it was surreal.

How could I, who, sixty minutes earlier, was tilting on the precipice of storyless nonbeing, now find myself sitting at a round table, talking with a forty-year-old, stay-at-home mother of four about the beauty of her marriage? How were authentic words about her husband and her embodying Jesus Christ and his radiant love for his people coming from *my* lips?

How was it that hope from the big, eternal Story was dancing inside of me at that moment?

WHEN *WHAT CAN BE* ISN'T ENOUGH

Growing up, I never had much use for pondering how things *would be* at the end of time (mine or anyone else's).

My faith had more or less centered on our human, God-shaped hole and Jesus' supernatural—and very helpful—capacity to fill it. I was very content with what could be in this life. Talking about eternity begged questions about future life and death, heaven and hell, and other socially awkward, seemingly ethereal concepts. So a quietly emergent "don't ask, don't tell" approach to the far bigger picture had left me with an unarticulated "Me + God = my best life now" theology, which seemed to be enough.

Until it wasn't.

A few years after my book on unintentional singleness came out, I was feeling burned out from all the travel and speaking. My organization granted me a sabbatical. A few months before it was to begin, my two-year-old nephew, Jude, drowned in my parents' pool. He was held alive by machines for one week, and that one week in pediatric ICU taught me that though we are designed by God to flourish in this world, sometimes—in shocking ways—it fails to happen. Even when care is excellent, faith is great, and the burden of prayer is carried around the world, life on this planet can be, simply, nipped in the bud.

When I'd gotten the news—a phone call telling me that Jude had drowned and to *come home now*—I couldn't breathe, and, stunned, I crumpled. I called dear friends who, graciously and despite my protests, met me at my house, packed up my bags, and drove me the two-plus hours to my hometown of Charlottesville.

When I walked into the kitchen, I was met by a host of women, my mom's friends, organizing food and manning the phone. And there were family members hugging, struggling in teary uncertainty. Even now, as I write this, I can feel the staggering weight of it all.

All that transpired with Jude confronted me with death, something that I, who still longed to create a *Sound of Music* life, had never faced so starkly. Death, particularly of a child, slaps you out of any illusions of invincibility. It sends your heart, soul, and mind spinning. Really, it blows up the universe—or makes you want to blow it up.

Gratefully, my organization got this. They extended my sabbatical, freeing up time for lots and lots of counseling and healing prayer (and not a little painting) to help me find my feet again. And over time, I did.

Here, though, is where I need to introduce you to "Tommy 4," as he'd been nicknamed by some family members. My older brother and sister-in-law's eldest son. The namesake of his father, grandfather, and great-grandfather. Tommy was my first nephew, and I was just flat-out crazy about him. I enjoyed *just being* with this tall, lanky, lovable boy. Since he was a baby, his winsome smile had come so easily.

Three years after Jude drowned, this beloved nineteen-year-old slipped off a roof, fell four stories, and died. There was no alcohol or drugs involved. Just fun-loving, college-student stargazing gone crushingly awry. Had I been college-age myself, I probably would have been on the rooftop too.

When I got the call about Tommy, just as with Jude, I collapsed. But then I looked up at God and told him directly, "No, not again. We will not have this in our family again. No." But my defiant no had proved a weak little protest in the face of the facts. And once again, just as with Jude, dear friends packed up my bags and drove me to Charlottesville.

About four months after Tommy fell, my parents and I were sitting on the white sands of Virginia Beach, our bodies splotchy red from uneven sunning. I watched as the beach-goers began winding down for the day. From our low-slung seats, our heels and toes toyed with the sand, and one of us opened the mini Igloo cooler. One raspberry soda was left.

"Let's toast Tommy 4," I suggested. "Let's declare his great points, the things we love." So as we sat in our little sandy circle, each of us made a declaration, lifted the can, took a sip, then passed it on.

"His big smile."

"And twinkly eyes."

"His capacity to bridge gaps between so many kinds of people."

"His tall, lumbering, gangly self!"

"His confidence."

"The way he'd take both my hands in his and lightly play with them."

And then my mother's eyes began watering. My heart clutched in my chest, even as I could hear my father try to suck back sniffles. There we sat, toes working sand, shoulders shaking up and down, lips quivering. Each of us now lost in our own thoughts of this first grandson, whose gripless docksiders had slipped on the black-iced roof.

If Jude's shocking death taught me about life ending, the sudden loss of Tommy 4 did something more. It catapulted me into questions of eternity that had just not mattered before.

I began scouring the Scriptures for words about death, resurrection, heaven, hell. I picked up books and read. I talked to people. And slowly, I began to suspect—*this is real.* I mean, I'd always thought words about new heavens and a new earth to come were technically true, but that had been in an abstract way . . . like how you might know the names of presidents or the periodic table or the quadratic formula. I accepted eternity as an idea, part of a spiritual equation that had little to do with real-life experience.

When Jude died, his father told me that it was as if his arm had been ripped off his body and sent straight up to heaven. That, my brother said, turned his attention to a place he might have previously ignored. When Tommy 4 died, his father's voice was snatched from him for a very long time. Grief can do that.

For me, these two staggering losses (plus the ongoing backdrop of missing marriage) in a sense forced my face into the mud. But instead of suffocating in the mix, I found myself slowly pushed through—helped by deep, repeated dives into counseling and prayer—into a different place. Up I came, spitting dirt and twigs out of my mouth. Wiping clear my eyes, over the course of about five years, I began to see that my little life on this planet was a small (albeit important and much loved) piece in a far greater story.

Accompanying me in that discovery was the book of Job in the Old Testament, one of the most well-known explorations of suffering in Scripture. Job, the protagonist, loses his family, his wealth, and his health—all with God's knowledge and permission.

My friend Michael suggested one time that, as with Job, the things that I had feared and dreaded had in fact come upon me. He encouraged me to dwell deeply with this man who had suffered so greatly. And as I read the last chapters of Job again and again, my heart began to know, in a way that felt almost three-dimensional in its solidity, *Yes, Job is right. There really is a God of angels and stars, all of whom sang together before I or Jude or Tommy 4 entered this planet.*[106] Breath came back to me slowly as I began to realize, *There really is a God who contains the power of the seas, including the waves of emotion that have been crashing over me for months upon months upon months.*[107] *There really is a God who knows the gates of death and depths of darkness, including that which I—and so many of my family members—have fallen into.*[108]

And I saw that though the world, the flesh, and the devil still work their sorcery, God is and was and always shall be in control. In a way deeper than ever before, I found myself

---

[106] Job 38:7.
[107] Job 26:12.
[108] Job 38:17.

saying with Job to God, "I had heard of you by the hearing of the ear, but now my eye sees you."[109]

In the midst of my wrestling with Scripture, the ideas of *death* and *resurrection* began to gain new traction inside of me. Jude died. Tommy died. But what if I really was going to see them again? What if the angel who had declared centuries before to the two grieving women, "Do not be afraid, for I know that you seek Jesus who was crucified. He is not here, for he has risen, as he said" was actually right?[110]

What if the dead, like Jesus, could rise? And what if the apostle Paul was right when he spoke of Jesus one day returning to raise all those who were in him into a new, tangible, bodily life?[111] A new life lived on a new earth set in a new heavens? What if, because of Jesus, death was really dead, once and for all? What if a new landscape of relationships and work and worship was actually opening up?

Jesus promised the thief who was about to die that he would be with him in paradise. What if Jude, who slipped into the pool, and Tommy, who slipped off the roof, had in fact slipped into paradise? Maybe this current life was not, nor was it intended to be, *the* bottom line. *The* end of the story.

✦ ✦ ✦

Less than twenty-four hours after I wrote the previous part of this chapter, I received a frantic phone call from my mother: "Connally, come home, now! I found Daddy on the

---

[109] Job 42:5.
[110] Matthew 28:5-6.
[111] Romans 8:9-11.

floor, and I think he's gone!" I—who had just earnestly written about the powerful beauty of the "big, eternal Story"—was now, shockingly, once again assaulted, this time by my father's sudden death by heart attack. We all know that older parents will one day die, but the out-of-the-blue-ness of the call felt too familiar—a breathtaking slap. And I collapsed on Paula's kitchen floor.

An hour later, Paula and her husband had packed my things and were driving me halfway to Charlottesville; other friends would meet us in the middle and carry me the rest of the way. Staring out that window as we drove, I knew I was hearing a whispered invitation. My father's death would mean a radical life change for my mother, married for fifty-six years—since age twenty-one. It would also mean the loss of our family home of forty years; a change of roles among us children, who lived on three continents; and very deep missing of a man whose smile of delight in me was a genuine gift to my heart.

The invitation was to walk into this host of looming changes, known and not, exchanging defiance for something of the interior solidity that had been born in the previous years. It was as if Jesus himself was whispering, *Now is the time to let your eternal hope play backward into your present journey.*

FREED FROM THE INVISIBLE BURDEN

A phone call, a collapse, a car ride. Truly a tough trio to keep repeating. I wouldn't wish this kind of shock (or any kind, for that matter) on anyone. It's the sort of thing that could keep you forever sitting in your chair, paralyzed, unable to risk running down the beach and diving into the beautiful sea ever again.

But can we discover a beautiful hope in the midst of such pain and sorrow? The answer is yes.

The question, though, for many of us, is *How?* How does this "hope playing backward" thing actually work? How can we reach into some unseen, ethereal future and grab hold of something solid enough to cling to in a very seen and felt, gritty, confusing current reality? How is it that hope from the big, eternal Story comes to dance inside us even in the most chaotic and hard, hard moments?

This is what I can tell you so far. Hope grows real as you are set free from the demand to "be all that you can be" and "live your best life now." I'm not suggesting that you embrace a slack mediocrity or a "whatever" posture to cut personal losses. Rather, I'm saying that the omnipresent command in our culture to self-actualize in order to find self-fulfillment comes with a shadowy flip side, a weighty burden, a strong undertow: You've got to be, get, and do it all, and stay pretty in the process.

Yet if, despite all your goals, labor, tears, and prayer, you miss your shot or, worse yet, the chance to take your shot never comes, what then?

What if, no matter how much you love children, you never get those babies?

What if that ideal husband, the answer to your prayers, actually turns out to be abusive or just perpetually withdrawn?

What if that hard-won degree never catapults you into the professional position that was promised?

What if loneliness silently eats your lunch even when your very best friends believe that you are living your dreams?

The prevailing answer? At best, it's often: *Try harder.* At worst: *Well . . . um . . . sorry.*

What I'm saying is that, in spite of our best efforts, brick walls drop in our path. There are inexorable dead-ends in this life that all the catchy clichés, or even powerful prayers, cannot or do not break through. There comes a time in everyone's life when loss, in some form or another, wins. That's really what death is—the loss that, for all we can see and feel, seems to win forever.

Paradoxically, freedom begins as we look such loss right in the eye, feel its burdensome weight, and acknowledge its temporary victory. For it is in the face of such undeniable loss that the beautiful, eternal goodness of Jesus Christ can begin to glimmer, perhaps with new brightness. When the light has gone out, the radiance of him who holds our right hand[112] can begin to flicker, maybe even glow. He is the one apart from whom there is, as the psalmist David wrote, "no good thing."[113] He is the one who will not abandon you or me "to the realm of the dead." Undaunted by the darkest shadows, he makes known to you and me the "path of life," bringing with him the promise of "eternal pleasures."[114]

---

[112] Isaiah 41:13.
[113] Psalm 16:12, NIV.
[114] Psalm 16:10-11, NIV.

A Related Aside

At this point, in talking about missing out and loss, I realize that I would be remiss if I didn't pause for a moment and mention the topic of sex. One of the ongoing pushbacks I've received, personally as well as in messages from the culture at large, is that in embracing a positive, Christian sexual ethic, I've actually chosen an unnecessary death of sorts. A pleasure-stopping dead-end of my own making. For we're at this strange societal juncture where if one forgoes having sex, even for the sake of integrity and deep conviction (like believing sex is meant for marriage), it's tantamount to saying one is living a "B-grade" or "JV" life. In the medieval era, celibacy might have come with a badge of honor. Now, it seems to indicate a psychological problem.

I remember taking a ticket from a client at the food bank where I volunteered. He noticed my ringless left hand, looked me up and down, whistled, and declared with a head shake, "Now, that's a waste." Then he continued with what was actually a winsome, knowing chuckle, "If the boys you meet aren't up to it, I can help you put all of that to good use." He winked, I laughingly thanked him for his kind offer, shook my head no, and sent him to the canned-goods section.

For most of my adult life, as a single woman, I've wrestled with questions of what to do with my sexual energy. "Oh, God," I've prayed. "Please don't let me lose my estrogen before my virginity!"

You may laugh. But when almost every message around

me screams that orgasm is life's consummate pleasure, I've struggled to believe that our culture is wrong.

And let's be honest, I've probably been missing out on a very good thing. But what if this good thing, sex, isn't actually god? Not the ultimate source of deliverance, healing, and life? In the best case, a loving sexual relationship can be a beautifully life-giving and pleasurable gift of God, our creator, bringing deep oneness, strong bonds, and maybe babies into a marriage. And sometimes, it seems to offer a taste of transcendence, a sneak peek into something of what is to come eternally (that is, at least, what they tell me). But what if, still, it is not *the source* of salvation?

Truthfully, for most of my twenties and thirties, I suspected that to live as a celibate single woman would be like embracing some form of pointless death. I feared I'd end up as some tired, beleaguered, pleasureless, sandpapery whiff of smoke. Dramatic, but you get the idea. But as I've gone along (making my share of mistakes in the journey), I've been the most surprised of all to discover that though I've neither been married nor had sex, *I'm not dead*. My life hasn't faded into the dullness of an old beige sweater. I'm the shocked one!

What repeatedly threatened to be a life-stopping brick wall has in fact turned out—retrospectively—to be a riverbank. In risking following Jesus' lead, the waters of my desire have been constrained, gathered to gush out in life-giving ways. In my wildest dreams, I never would have imagined that in the face of what has felt, at times, like genuinely missing out, such rich fruit could be borne. I'm embarrassed to say that it has taken me roughly thirty years to actually recognize this. Along the way, my willingness to obey (faithfulness) has definitely been stronger than my trust (faith-filledness), but I simply cannot deny what I've come to see.

Real Freedom

All of this is to say, the burden of loss—from small, unmet desires to raging, ripping death; from real pleasures forgone to even the pressure to see fruit borne from the pain—such burdens can be desperately real but do not have to be omnipotent. This is because, as Job and Revelation and a hundred other biblical passages flesh out, the Good News shouts a different tale. It is possible to make peace with things that aren't (or may, honestly, never be in this life) because there really is a—dare I say *the*—consummation still to come. It's possible to face and continue to feel loss—even irrevocable loss at the level of shocking death, quietly missing out, or something in between—*and also* live a life dripping with meaning, love, and color.

Our lives on this planet are of inestimable value to God. Why else would he show up here, for us, as one of us, sharing in even our tears? But life on this planet, with its rich experiences and devastating losses, is not the whole story. As we lay hold of this far bigger vision of reality, with its renewed heavens and earth still to come, we find a new freedom.

The panorama opens up, and it's as if the best parts of this life, our most cherished longings, and our sweetest moments (including the most God-blessed sexual encounters), are seen for what they really are: not the consummate meal that, if cooked and consumed, will satisfy all hungers, but a round of wonderfully delicious hors d'oeuvres. And these hors d'oeuvres are mysteriously offered by a very real divine Host, pointing to a wedding banquet with himself that waits for us behind currently shut doors. There is a consummation still to come, and no matter the extent of my missing, my loss, my brick walls, or the inevitable fact of death itself, I have not been cheated out of consummate pleasure. Really.

Every now and then, I stop and envision a banquet with those we love who have followed Jesus into this party. Even as I write this, I can picture my father with his winsome smile, proudly introducing Tommy 4 and Jude to his own father, who died when my dad was a teen. "Daddy," my father says, "meet your great-grandsons!" And there are twinkly eyes, smiles, and back-slapping hugs all around as—I know this is a mystery—they wait together in Christmas Eve-esque anticipation for the wedding banquet to begin.

The irrevocable losses in my life or yours, from others' choices or our own, might be painfully real and insurmountable. But they don't mean that there isn't a more real and grander-still intimacy to come, rich fruit still to be borne. For those who are in Jesus, death cannot, ultimately, stop the eternal flourishing for which we are designed. I've actually begun to know, in a way that carries emotional weight, that the future—on this planet and beyond—holds the promise of infinitely great memories still to be made.

This brings me courage. It can bring you courage, too. I'm talking about the courage that opens you to receive a freeing shift right in the middle of the thing you are missing most. It's the courage that allows you, even in the presence of loss, to keep looking forward. For as hard as opening your gaze to the future without *it* or *him* or *her* can be, grounded in the weighty promise of *what will be*, with the presence of Jesus Christ dwelling within you, you can find the courage to risk discovering how God's goodness is still showing up, even today.

Reflections on

HOW HOPE PLAYS BACKWARD

1. Can you describe a moment in your life where the reality of Jesus Christ shone irrefutably clear to you? If so, what did it feel like? What, if anything, shifted in you as a result of such an encounter? If no specific moment comes to mind, simply describe in general terms how Jesus has revealed himself to you. What has that been like? If you have yet to encounter Jesus, what about him intrigues you?

2. For all of the goodness that is available to you in this life through the redeeming power of Jesus Christ, sometimes that which you long for the most proves repeatedly, or even permanently, elusive. Sometimes the *can be* isn't enough. Read Job 3:20-26. "What I feared," Job laments, "has come upon me" (NIV). He speaks candidly of his sighing, groanings, dis-ease, and trouble. What aspects of Job's groaning can you identify with? In what areas of your own life have you hit insurmountable brick walls? How has this affected you? How has it affected your vision and trust of Jesus Christ?

3. When you hear someone encourage you to "be all that you can be," how does this affect you? Do you find it motivational, burdensome, other? Try explaining why this is. How could knowing that (no matter how gifted or committed you are) it is impossible to have a perfect life actually be a source of relief?

4. What, if any, consideration have you given to the reality of an eternal future, including new heavens and a new earth, with Jesus Christ and his people? Does such a promise seem distant and remote? Energizing and empowering? Somewhere in between? How might a more personal and robust grasp of eternity bring greater freedom into your present circumstances? In what areas of your life do you need this greater freedom?

5. Read Revelation 19:6-10. What does the passage say about the Lord? What does it say about the "marriage supper"? Why might the author, John of Patmos, have chosen this image of a marriage supper to describe what awaits God's people? Imagine yourself there for a moment. What might it be like? What might it feel like? How might such a vision bring you hope in your current, day-to-day life?

CHAPTER 9

AND YET, UNDAUNTED

Living Well in the Unfinished Symphony

The best gift you and I can receive as followers of Jesus Christ, this side of heaven, is the bedrock confidence that our story is playing into an eternal drama where the victory is already won. Death is *not* the final story. This is the "stuff" that keeps us going—undaunted.

But we know, too, that such an eternal vision with its empowering promise is not always easy for contemporary, present-tense people like us to apprehend. We've got a world of anesthesia, analgesia, and a host of other life-management tools. We're just not prone to look into the consummate future to find real emotional strength, let alone direction for today. My friend who lived in Russia for seventeen years puts it this way: "America has so much artificial light, honestly, sometimes the light of Jesus just seems to pale."

In truth, a lot of us Jesus followers simply need a hand to begin apprehending, in ever-more-real ways, the beauty and power of our promised future. Washing into our lives like waves rolling in from another universe, glimpses of eternity can bring a hope that strengthens us at a gut level. But how do we learn to really surf these waves?

GOD'S STORYBOARD

Paula

The prophet Isaiah has an uncanny ability to encourage the fainthearted, though I should note it's ironic that it's also rumored that he met with a rather bad end (sawn in half). I love the man for many reasons. He wrote to people like us—people who lived in exile with little memory of the Garden past or hope in God's glorious future.

Isaiah 53 tells of a Man of Sorrows, "acquainted with grief," on whom was laid the iniquity of us all. This is the one who would one day, for all time, open the way back to God. This is the one who would finally deliver God's people into the future they longed for.

You can hear this part of Isaiah's message in any Christian church at Easter. What you won't hear, necessarily, is the next part, in Isaiah 54. How does God stoop to reveal his glorious future played back into life as you and I encounter it in the present moment? Who does he choose to storyboard this drama so that his current *and* future redemption takes on flesh and blood we can recognize?

Why, the pictures of the most unlikely women you can imagine! In fact, I dare say it's women whose lives we fear could be ours if something big fell apart. You could call these women our "worst nightmares," and yet, their reality may be the bad dream in which we find ourselves. In fact, these women are so universal they could be found in any culture, any time. They could be sitting on the bus next to you. They could be you.

So if hope can bloom undaunted here . . . well, it can bloom in a thousand chaotic places in your life and ours. And this, we believe, is why God chose to storyboard his eternal hope through the lives of these women, much as Jesus chose to make his resurrection known first to Mary Magdalene.

These four women need an introduction, though. First, Isaiah speaks of the "barren" woman, who, for different reasons in every life phase, never holds her own children in her arms. This is a loss that woman feels in the core of her being. Second, there's the woman who carries the "shame of [her] youth" with her. She's forgiven, yes, but perhaps, years later, she is still trying to undo the effects of earlier choices.

Then Isaiah speaks of the plight of a woman who is more familiar, "the reproach of your widowhood." With her husband gone, she has lost her place in the scheme of things. She faces life alone, perhaps for the first time. And the fourth woman: "a wife deserted . . . a wife of youth when she is cast off." How many women have known the desolation of being traded in for another by the men they love?

I don't know about you, but my stomach rather knots up when I picture any of these scenarios. I realize how much of my invisible energy goes into avoiding *exactly this*. But then, as we've said throughout this book . . . life happens while you are busy making other plans. (Okay. We stole that from John Lennon, but it's totally true).[115]

So, really, we are all ears to hear how God takes his eternal *what will be*, all this glory and promise to come, and dribbles it into the worst cracks of a woman's existence. How do we pull the promise into the actual reality of what we might be living right now?

Isaiah's first word to us in this passage is *sing*.[116]

If we lift our eyes to see that the broken shards of the story we are living now will come together in some way that shows the actual glory of God, if we could "see" that this is not the end of the story . . . honestly, wouldn't we break into song? Could we not help but sing?

Well, Isaiah is essentially saying, *Honey, dance your jig and sing now.* And let the song lift you to the only hope that does not disappoint.[117]

I have to say that I often find this something of a conscious choice. Toward the end of my mother's life, I'd visit her and frequently find her lying on her bed, facing the wall, resting or asleep. My vibrant, work-circles-around-me mother, lying on the bed in the middle of the afternoon, facing a wall.

---

[115] From John Lennon, "Beautiful Boy (Darling Boy)," *Double Fantasy* © 1980 Geffen: "Life is what happens to you while you're busy making other plans."
[116] Isaiah 54:1.
[117] Romans 5:5, NASB.

This depressing picture stopped me in my tracks. I wanted to run out the door.

I tried to remind myself that there had also been a few small miracles in her later years. Her battle with alcohol had driven her places she swore she'd never go—a local women's Bible study, for example. I will never forget her phone call to tell me what a good teacher the leader was (and my mother would recognize a good teacher), and even more important, this woman often wore clothes from my mother's favorite store, Talbots. My jaw fell to the floor. I think I mumbled something about how I hoped that helped her Bible teaching. But what I thought was, *Dear God, you will use anything*. That Bible study and those gracious women stitched my mother together for seven years, long after she got many of her answers right.

Here she was, though, nearing the end of it all, sleeping in the daytime, facing the wall. I would stand in her doorway, take a deep breath, and make myself remember what was real that could not be seen.

This wall was, at some point, going to crack wide open, and my mother, young and whole and beautiful, was going to step out into a scene more lovely than the emerald hills of Ireland. That was reality. As I stood there, little threads of peace—and even joy—would weave themselves into me. Often, I'd find myself praying that God, in his mercy, would transform the affliction of her latter years into spiritual blessing in the lives of her great-grandchildren.

I could, then, sit down and talk with this declining woman who was facing the end of her earthly story. Or the end of our stories together. When she died a few months later, that was my first thought: *My mother is indeed walking beautiful green hills.*

I think this is what the writer of Hebrews was trying to tell us in some of the most dramatic words of the New Testament.[118] He wrote that we haven't come to this cold, blazing mountain where everyone stands terrified waiting for judgment. No, we've come to the City of the Living God, where the angels are decked out in their party clothes, and there in the crowd are actual people we've loved—and most of all, Jesus awaits us. Heaven is an already-happening thing.

The metaphor I return to, time and again, is one that C. S. Lewis coined. He said that there in heaven, right now, the symphony is playing, full bore, filling every corner with wildly upgraded Bach. But of course, the problem is that we aren't quite there. We are sitting in a kitchen here, in front of an old radio spitting out a grainy melody that's hard to follow, mere faint threads of the symphony that is, indeed, playing now in all its glory.[119]

PULLING THE FUTURE INTO THE PRESENT

Connally

When I read what Paula wrote about singing, my mind leapt to a song made famous by Mahalia Jackson, who was known in her day as the "Queen of Gospel." I've often listened to the old recordings, trying to sing along. Her voice is rich, velvety,

---

[118] Hebrews 12:18-22.
[119] Best described in *Miracles*, C. S. Lewis (1942).

powerful. She bends and plays with notes; they're like putty in her hands. "I sing," she croons from some deep well where God's goodness long before seeped in, "I sing because I'm happy; I sing because I'm free, for his eye is on the sparrow, and I know he watches me."[120]

How can such simple words carry so much weight?

The Queen of Gospel used to say that singing was an expression of her hope—but also brought her the gift of hope.[121] This is the crazy, two-sided mystery in this word *sing* that Isaiah offers to us. On one hand, a divine somebody else has unleashed deliverance in our lives. Someone else is carrying the weight of all the brokenness until everything is made right—which it will be. There is a reason for hope; our spirits alight. A song of response rising up within makes all the sense in the world.

Yet because we are not quite there, sometimes we sing simply to inhabit the hope of what is promised. We sing, and keep singing, until that hope makes its way down into the crooks and crevices of our still-to-be-made-right lives. We sing by faith, and as we do, hope pours in, lifting our eyes.

The evening after my dad's memorial service, family and a few friends from out of town gathered at my mother's house. People were finishing up dinner when my uncle, a longtime rock 'n' roller, dusted off my somewhat out-of-tune guitar and started strumming. Everyone slowly made his or her way

---

[120] "His Eye Is on the Sparrow" (lyrics by Sivily D. Martin). In 2010, Jackson won a Grammy for her 1958 single of this song (by Columbia Records).
[121] Jim Irvin and Colin McLear, eds., *The Mojo Collection: The Ultimate Music Companion*, 4th ed. (Edinburgh: Canongate Books, 2003), 20.

into the den—sitting on sofas or cross-legged on the floor, some still in funeral finery, some in well-worn jeans.

Then we began to sing. We sang the Beatles; we sang the blues. We sang great hits, and we sang hymns. Nobody knew all the words to every song, not even my dear uncle. But oh, how we sang. Voices blended, mostly, as we tried to bend and play with notes. More hymns. More harmonies.

I cannot quite explain what transpired that night. It was like we were singing with the exuberance that was now my dad's and one day would be ours. And as we sang, faces streaked earlier with tears now grew flush with—dare I say?— very present joy. In spite of death, in spite of all the sadness in that room, which would not be solved that night or the next, the heavens parted. Grief—from the loss of my father but also the accumulated losses in generations of lives—had clutched so many hearts, but that evening, for a few timeless moments, the happiness and freedom were palpable.

"Sing!" says Isaiah to those of us who are willing to risk believing that our lives sit within a bigger Story. To those women who are slugging through the worst and even the very best that life can bring, to us, the old prophet calls, "Sing now!" Sing to the God of *what will be*, pulling the future into the present, buttressed by the hope of *what will be*.

The singing, though, is only the beginning. Because we are guaranteed of *what will be*, we actually are beckoned to *do something now*. "Enlarge the place of your tent," Isaiah says. "Let the curtains of your habitations be stretched out; do not hold back."[122]

---

[122] Isaiah 54:2.

Because barrenness will never be the final end of the story, this woman who seems to have drawn the short straw in this life is called to throw cynical self-protection to the wind. Deliverance has been unleashed, and she whose dreams have collapsed is called to build.

Build? I mean, who says that to a barren woman? Who says, "Build a bigger house because the generations that are going to flow from your barren body are going to people desolate cities!"? Perhaps the only one who can say it with any authority is the one who sees something we can't.

Can you imagine, just for a moment, what you might do—right now—if you could trust that that one recurringly nightmarish place in your life will one day be made right? What if you knew that one day, things would be set right between you and your sister? What would you do if you knew that one day, the injustice you experienced would be fully seen and set right? What might change if the broken promise that broke your heart didn't have the final say?

What would I do today if I knew that my ongoing single-ness didn't mean being cut out for eternity from the best intimacy a human being could know? Truthfully, I think I'd snap a little more quickly out of my victim bent. I'd stand up a little straighter. Mostly, I'd go ahead and take those tango lessons I've always quietly envisioned.

Paula would say that her version of "stretching out" has played out a little differently. It's more the story of how God has scooped up the pile of her grief and reshaped it into something she hardly recognizes. About the point in life when most people would wind things down, suddenly, out of nowhere, new passions have emerged. Doors unseen before have flung open. "Stretch out" and "build" look like moving in a direction she never thought about before.

For Paula, a family infertility story has introduced her to a whole fraternity of people concerned about the plight of at-risk kids—and lots of couples seeking to adopt or foster children. It has given her a chance to write about the attachment needs of these children and the importance of finding either stable family members or stable homes of permanency sooner, so that children aren't trapped in a broken system they can't escape.

You may recognize this theme in your own life, if you think about it. Life hits you in the face, as it did for the women in Isaiah's passage. You are tempted to permanently trim your sails and seek safe harbor where nothing can touch you again. But you hear the music in the distance, and you know the promise of something happening that's a whole lot more important than your own well-being. It frees you up to fight for tastes of that goodness on planet Earth, now.

Yes, life in this world is hard. And grief can make you bitter. Maybe you feel that hot breath of bitterness breathing down your neck. But grief can also make you braver and bolder. And if the victory is already won and the party is this minute in full swing, then put on your purple hat and head into the wind with your head up. Let God bloom new passion from the ashes of your lost dreams, because he specializes in that.

Of all people, you are the woman who can "laugh at the days to come."[123]

---

[123] This is the actual translation of Proverbs 31:25, NIV.

FEAR NOT

Paula

Isaiah tells us to sing and let the song carry us. Because the goodness of the *end* is already settled, he encourages us to move forward, stretching out and building in some new way that requires faith. But then, rather unexpectedly, Isaiah doubles back. It's like he suddenly remembers who he's talking to—and who he's talking to are people very much like you and me.

He seems to know we never get far in any direction without confronting a familiar dragon: *fear.*

I mean, didn't you honestly think you would outgrow your fears and anxieties? Didn't you believe you'd learn enough Bible verses, read enough books like this one, and gather enough supportive friends that you could forever tip-toe past its grasping claws?

I guess that's why Isaiah is someone I look forward to meeting on the other side. It's the reason the pages of his writing are falling out of my Bible. He's such a lover of God and such a realist about human nature. He knows that even as we move toward this glorious eternal hope, we carry some anxiety with us in our suitcases—because we are not yet home.

The picture Isaiah paints is one where the fear of things falling apart—yes, the fear is there—doesn't control the show. He promises that we won't be left in shame and disgrace. We will hardly be able to remember those times we felt undone. That's Isaiah's reassurance to anxious women who are staking everything on a hope that transcends potential nightmares.

Isaiah says that the reason you can't give in to being controlled by fear is a deeply relational one. He doesn't appeal to the Law or the Prophets or the comfort of David's psalms. No, he moves into the most intimate space of your life, up close where you long to be cared for by someone who won't ever let you go:

> For your Maker is your husband,
>   the LORD of hosts is his name;
> and the Holy One of Israel is your Redeemer,
>   the God of the whole earth he is called.[124]

As a woman married to a good man for more than forty years, I can appreciate that when Isaiah wants to personify human love at its most profound, he reaches for "husband." I am a woman who has tasted the rich goodness of marriage.

I'm also in a position to appreciate what Isaiah is saying here: As close as you think any human relationship can be in your life, there is one closer. *Your Maker is your husband.* The Lord of hosts has moved in with you. The God of the whole earth has your back, honey. And this is the ultimate reason why you can actually step into pieces of God's eternal hope now.

Isaiah's words here have been some of the most stabilizing ones of my adult life. Only the way I figure it, if this is true about a relationship with one's husband, then it follows for every relationship that matters. In those moments when

---

[124] Isaiah 54:5.

human beings fail and I feel the sharp stab of that failure, I make myself stop. I have my own little litany on this. And I can't tell you how much it helps.

Lord, I thank you that my Maker is my husband and my brother, my father and my mother, my closest friend, the lover of my soul. Yes, you are the lover of my soul.

I don't think I'm stretching things too far. I see this as God's eternal hope playing back into the crevices of the relationships that matter most (and about which I'm most tempted to fear). My Maker, my Husband has me, and I will never, ever be left alone.

MOUNTAINS

Connally

Paula and I have written much of this book while together in the mountains of North Carolina. As we look off the deck of the house where we write, there is a mountainscape eight ridges deep—green turning into blue turning into gray. These are old mountains, worn down with time. But these mountains are solid, reliable, comforting simply to gaze on.

Isaiah, I am 99.9 percent sure, did not have our beloved Blue Ridge Mountains in mind as he wrote chapter 54. The mountains he must have known were those scattered throughout Israel. Jerusalem itself had been built on a mountain.

But what he did know was that for his audience, the exiled Hebrew people, their mountains had crumbled. Their culture had been shredded, they had been taken captive, Mount Zion was far gone from their sight.

And to this group of people, whose complete restoration God promised, Isaiah declared,

> "For the mountains may depart
> and the hills be removed,
> but my steadfast love shall not depart from you,
> and my covenant of peace shall not be removed,"
> says the LORD, who has compassion on you.[125]

Think for a moment of the mountains with which you are most familiar. What would happen inside you if they crumbled? Literally, what might watching that—even from a distance—feel like in your body? What would happen to your breath? It's hard for me to imagine those eight mountain ridges in North Carolina literally melting down. But if something so strong, so solid, so replete with that quality of "foreverness" were to collapse, so would my heart.

Honestly, for my whole family, losing Jude, then Tommy, then my dad has been like mountains crumbling. In some ways, these kinds of profound losses are like the very cells in our bodies turning to dust and being washed away by a sea of adrenaline.

But the words of Isaiah 54—about the love of the Lord standing in the face of collapse—have branded themselves in me. My energy grows when I get to write and speak about

---

[125] Isaiah 54:10.

the reality of eternity. I take such joy from this. Discovering at a gut level *what will be* brings me tremendous courage.

> *Though my knight in shining armor never shows up,*
> *though my brothers live forever overseas, though another*
> *sudden death happens, though this book is a bust and*
> *my speaking gigs dry up, though I'm not gotten by*
> *certain people like I long to be, though I flirt with fear*
> *throughout my journey . . . the Lord's steadfast love, his*
> *covenant commitment, and his compassion will never*
> *stop. Never.*

Sometimes, when my hope is wavering, when I'm feeling lonely or I'm a bit scared by the unknowns of my future, I sing these words from Isaiah. Literally. I sing them. And as Mahalia Jackson says, my hope grows. Oh, boy, Isaiah really does know what even redeemed people whose future is secure need.

At the start of this book, we said that we wanted you to trek with us through the terrain of God's Larger Story. As Paula and I sit on this deck, processing all the ways in which God has revealed himself in our respective journeys so far, we both know that we are not yet fully living in what is to come. There are mountain ranges still ahead.

Isaiah rounds out his beautiful chapter 54 with words about a city, a new Jerusalem that will be made with precious stones. Those who have been storm tossed will find themselves living with generations of others in peace—protected, vindicated, free.

I read the prophet's words, and I hear foreshadowing of the book of Revelation, written almost a thousand years later by John of Patmos. Revelation paints a picture of the world to come where tears are no longer needed; evil is judged and cast out for keeps; authority reigns, just and tender; ethnic tensions give way to honor; the nations are healed; beloved believers sing as the new heavens and earth come into being. And standing in the center of *what will be* is the glorious Son of Man.

Jesus Christ—the one who saw, loved, and received the tears of the sinful woman in front of the offended Pharisees. Our Maker and our Husband. The incarnation of our Father's goodness. The bright morning star whose face invites our loving gaze while lighting up this re-creation.

I smile when I ponder this. The vision of what is to come grows ever more tangible to me, like I could reach out and fill my water bottle in Jesus' springs of life. And yet . . . such a vision seems a million miles away from where I sit this moment—at a desk, on a rainy day, fighting a cold, wondering how I'll finish this chapter, prepare for tonight's "task force on ethnicity," *and* get in my workout at the Y.

John of Patmos ends the book of Revelation with Jesus' testimony that he is coming soon. Truthfully, neither Paula nor I have any real idea of what "soon" means. But when we step back and look at where we've journeyed in our lives and even in this book, we believe that the next stage of the journey will be worth the wait. We know that last mountain range opens up to panoramas beyond our wildest imaginations.

So between here and there, we've grown to believe that singing, stretching out, surrendering fear, again and again, makes total sense as we journey. Maybe you've gotten glimpses of this as well. Maybe you even want to join us as we blend our voices with John of Patmos's. He ends his book of Revelation with the words that hundreds upon hundreds of thousands have earnestly prayed as they, too, have waited: "Come, Lord Jesus!"[126]

Meanwhile, as we wait, we know that there is much good work to do and many people to love.

And though it's a bit daunting, I suspect it really might be a good idea to take that tango lesson.

---

[126] Revelation 22:20.

Reflections

on

AND YET, UNDAUNTED

1. Read Isaiah 54:1-8. When telling of what redemption will look like (in flashes now, and one day, completely), Isaiah points to the transformed lives of four women: the barren woman, the woman carrying the shame of her youth, the unseen widow, and the wife who was deserted. Use your imagination for a moment. With which, if any, of these women can you identify? Explain the connection. What redemption is brought to each woman? How might the knowledge of the redemption that is offered to each woman bring you hope in your life?

2. Isaiah wrote to people in exile who had little memory of the Garden past or hope in God's glorious future. In what way(s), if any, do you sense you are living in exile? What is this like for you? How might a memory of the Garden past be a gift to you right now? And how could in hope of God's glorious future reshape those areas of your life where you feel, personally or culturally, you are in exile?

3. Isaiah invites, even exhorts, us to "sing!" Sometimes we sing as an overflow of our joy and trust; sometimes we sing because our hearts are dry and thirsty. In what way(s) have you sung for

either of these reasons? What was that like? How might singing to God actually transform your knowledge of and trust in him?

4. Isaiah encourages his listeners to stretch out, to build. Think of the four women—it does not matter what your story has been to this point; unseen doors can still be flung open! In what area(s) of your life might God be calling you to risk stretching out? To risk building or creating something new? How willing are you to listen and respond to this call?

5. Isaiah knows us! He knows that fear almost always nips at our heels. Rarely can we kick it away permanently. But we also need not let it steer our course. What fear(s) do you need—perhaps for the first time, perhaps for the hundredth time—to leave in Jesus' hands, that you might be about his business? What will it take for you to do this? As you give your fear up to him, what is the Lord offering you in return?

6. Take a few moments and read aloud all of Isaiah 54. Isaiah declares that though the mountains may fall and the hills turn to dust, yet the love of the Lord will stand. His covenant with us is immovable. His compassion is real. As you look at the chapter as a whole, how is the love of God revealed here? Now, look forward into the immediacy of your life on this planet, as well as into future fulfillment of the far Larger Story. What might it mean to you that no matter what, his love will be with you?

7. Spend time thanking God for the far Larger Story in which you find yourself. Ask him, in light of this big Story, what his simple next step might be for you in the journey. Listen for his answer. Tell someone. And then risk going forward, with his presence, yet undaunted.